Following the Curve of Time
The Legendary M. Wylie Blanchet

CATHY CONVERSE

Victoria • Vancouver • Calgary

TouchWood Editions
#108–17665 66A Avenue
Surrey, BC V3S 2A7
www.touchwoodeditions.com

TouchWood Editions
PO Box 468
Custer, WA
98240-0468

Library and Archives Canada Cataloguing in Publication

Converse, Cathy, 1944–
Following the curve of time : the life of M. Wylie Blanchet / Cathy Converse.

Includes bibliographic references and index.
ISBN 978-1-894898-68-3 (bound).—ISBN 978-1-894898-81-2 (pbk.)

1. Blanchet, M. Wylie (Muriel Wylie), 1891-1961. 2. Travel writers—British Columbia—Biography. 3. Travel writers—Canada—Biography. 4. Vancouver Island (B.C.)—Biography. 5. Women—British Columbia—Biography. 6. Inside Passage—Description and travel. 7. Pacific Coast (B.C.)—Description and travel. I. Title.

FC3844.25.B52C65 2008   971.1'203092   C2007-907439-1

LIBRARY OF CONGRESS CONTROL NUMBER: 2008921284

Edited by Marlyn Horsdal
Proofread by Meaghan Craven
Book design and layout by Ruth Linka
Cover photographs: Main photo by Cathy Converse. Inset photo Capi in rowboat, 1944.
COURTESY JANET BLANCHET

Printed in Canada by Friesens

BRITISH COLUMBIA
ARTS COUNCIL

Canada Council   Conseil des Arts
for the Arts   du Canada

TouchWood Editions acknowledges the financial support for its publishing program from the Government of Canada through the Book Publishing Industry Development Program (BPIDP), Canada Council for the Arts, and the province of British Columbia through the British Columbia Arts Council and the Book Publishing Tax Credit.

This book has been produced on 100% post-consumer recycled paper, processed chlorine free and printed with vegetable-based dyes.

For Brian
✣ ✣ ✣

Come run with me along the sea
When dusk sits on the land,
And search with me,
For shells are free,
And treasures hide in sand.
— Virginia Covey Boswell

This page: The *Caprice* at anchor in Welcome Pass, with the *Ivanhoe* in the background. COURTESY JANET BLANCHET

CONTENTS ⊹

ACKNOWLEDGEMENTS ✛

One of my great joys in writing this book was the wonderful people I met along the way. The book could not have been written without their assistance and I am very grateful for their support. I would like to thank Janet Blanchet, who never tired of my request for "just one more question." She answered countless queries that I had about her mother-in-law, M. Wylie "Capi" Blanchet, and she did so with grace, honesty and trust. A very special thank you goes to Tom Liffiton, who is related to Capi (Liffiton was her family name) and has researched the genealogy of the Liffiton family. He spent the better part of a year helping me gather information about Capi's early life. Among many things, he went through ships' records, transcribed illegible family letters, combed through burial records and found business records and family photographs taken by the noted photographer, William Notman of Montreal. I am greatly appreciative of the help that my husband, Brian Silvester, gave me. I know that authors always thank their family members, with good reason, but Brian is, in addition to being supportive, a master mariner and his assistance with the marine-related aspects of the book was indispensable. Marine terminology, in particular, is very precise and many times he rescued me from mixing up the colloquial with the correct. I am indebted to Rolf Hicker of www.hickerphoto.com for the photographs he so generously loaned to me for this publication. Rolf is a very talented nature and travel photographer of national and international repute.

There are two instances of help that warmed my faith in human kindness. In *The Curve of Time*, Capi mentioned an incident from her childhood in Cacouna, Quebec. I did not think the Liffitons had had a house there but I wondered about her grandfather Snetsinger. I had only an undated envelope, possibly from around 1911, with the word Cacouna written on it—not much to go on. I contacted Viateur Beaulieu, the web master for the Cacouna web site. Viateur did not know of any such house but searched around and not only found a reference to the "Snetsinger Villa," but went out in the winter's snow, and then again in the spring, to take pictures of the house for me. My heartfelt thanks also go to Rick Terrell, the park facility operator for Desolation Sound Marine Park, who similarly went beyond the call of duty when he took a boat across Desolation Sound into Prideaux Haven to find, at the remnants of "Mike's place," some stonework that I had been unable to discover on my last visit there.

I am grateful to Peter Macnair, who took time out of a very busy schedule to go over Capi's photographs of First Nations places and artifacts with me, and also to Dan Savard, the senior collections manager of audio-visual records for the Royal BC Museum. I would also like to thank Dr. Tim Yeomans, who helped me understand some of the medical aspects of this book, and Richard Blanchet for information about his father, Peter. Thanks also to Rosemary Joy, whose research on her family's genealogy included John Gray Goodall Snetsinger, Capi's maternal grandfather, and who helped provide information on Capi's background. She also graciously loaned me a few photographs. Yvonne Maximchuk, co-author of *Full Moon, Flood Tide,* answered numerous questions on Knight Inlet; Hugh Ackroyd, the Sunshine Coast area supervisor for BC Parks, responded to my inquiry on tourism and Desolation Sound; William Garden, naval architect, helped me understand boat design and told an interesting story about Capi; Edith Iglauer, who wrote an earlier article on Capi, responded to my many questions about her research. Thanks also to Rob Morris, editor of *Western Mariner*, Freda Thorne and Barbara Gilbert of the Sidney Museum Archives, Derek Hayes, author of several historical atlases, Tim McGrady of Knight Inlet Lodge and Valeria Cisotto for taking time to show me around The Latch, which is architecturally similar to Capi's "Little House." Gwyneth Hoyle, who has just completed a book about Geoffrey Blanchet's brother, *The Northern Horizons of Guy Blanchet*, provided information on the Blanchet family, and Mary Glezos found the Liffiton burial section for me at the Mount Royal Cemetery in Montreal. Finally, I would like to offer a special thank you to Bill and Donna Mackay, the owner-operators of Mackay Whale Watching who run the *Naiad Explorer* out of Port McNeill, for all their support in establishing contacts and for the insight and information they offered on the Broughton Archipelago.

VANCOUVER ISLAND

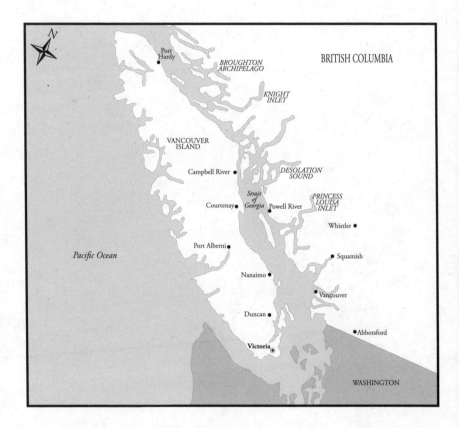

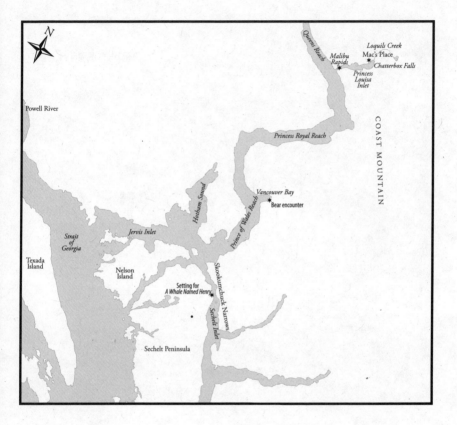

DESOLATION SOUND

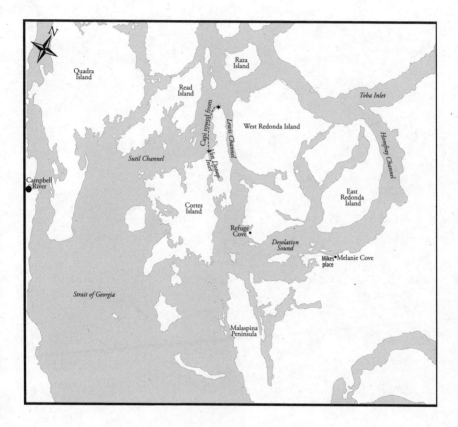

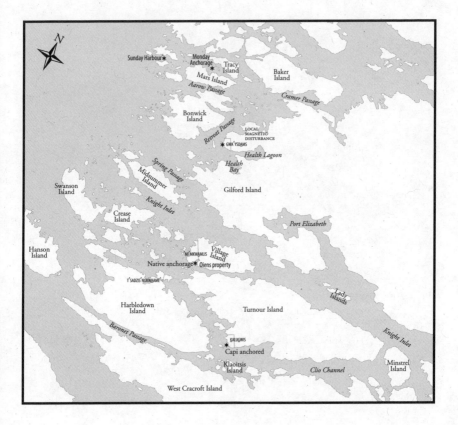

N

Sunday Harbour

Monday
Anchorage
Tracy
Island

Baker
Island

Mars Island

Aarow Passage

Cramer Passage

Bonwick
Island

Retreat Passage

LOCAL
MAGNETIC
DISTURBANCE

GWA'YSDAMS

Health Lagoon

Spring Passage

Health
Bay

Midsummer
Island

Swanson
Island

Knight Inlet

Gilford Island

Crease
Island

Port Elizabeth

Hanson
Island

MI'MKWAMLIS

Village
Island

Native anchorage

Ojens property

T'SADZIS'NUKWAAME'

Lady
Islands

Harbledown
Island

Turnour Island

Knight Inlet

Baronet Passage

ṈALUGWIS

Capi anchored

Clio Channel

Minstrel
Island

Klaoitsis
Island

West Cracroft Island

KNIGHT INLET

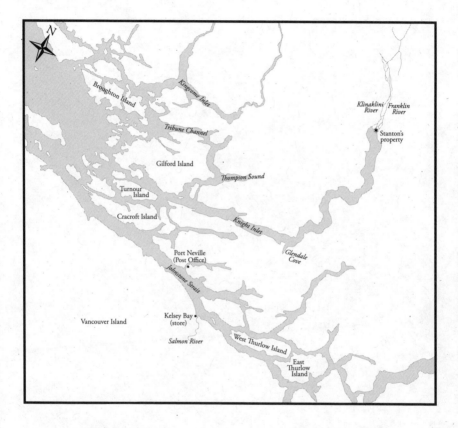

PREFACE ✢

When I was approached by Pat Touchie, my publisher, to write the biography of M. Wylie Blanchet, I was very excited. I have been writing about women's lives and accomplishments for the last thirty years and have always been concerned with the fact that women have been seen as a sidebar to our history, whereas the opposite is the reality. It has been a mission of mine to tell women's stories so that they may be appropriately woven into the fabric of British Columbia's history, but writing about Capi Blanchet was particularly thrilling for me for an additional reason. *The Curve of Time* has been in my library for at least twenty years and has accompanied me on many trips up and down the British Columbia coast. I love the book and have often referred to it in my travels. I have always lived along the shores of the Pacific Ocean and have spent years sailing this coast, but when my husband and I set out in *Ikkutut* in the summer of 2006 to revisit all of the places Capi had written about, I grew to appreciate her strong spirit even more. This book is meant as a tribute to her; it is in part biography and in part travelogue, offering an update on some of the places to which Capi takes readers in *The Curve of Time*.

The materials that are available to a biographer play an important part in shaping the resulting story. When I took on the task of writing a book about Capi Blanchet, I stepped into an abyss: there was little information available to guide me—no records kept, diaries written or memorabilia left. There was no archival information about her beyond vital statistics. Even Capi's place of birth was uncertain; some reports placed it in Montreal and others at Lachine, Quebec. Her early history was only twice alluded to in her book, and then only vaguely. I did have access to some of her photographs, a few letters written by her daughter Elizabeth and a genealogy of her maternal grandfather. There was an article about her by Edith Iglauer and, of course, her books. No one can stand outside a person's life and fully understand her heart, but with the help of those who came forward to tell me their recollections, I hope I have been able to offer a balance between the public and private dimensions of Capi's life. It was challenging, much like the woman herself. Capi Blanchet was an amazing person.

Capi Blanchet and *The Curve of Time*

Down a long, narrow, twisty country lane, bordered by stately maples, Douglas-firs, chartreuse-coloured arbutus trees and billowy-crowned shore pine, is a woodland area comprising some 2.5 hectares of rocky promontories, two small beaches and four hundred metres of waterfront with a stunning view of Sidney Island and snow-capped Mount Baker, the sentinel of the North Cascades. Slipping into a time before now, sixty-some years ago, a hiker in this area might have found a small clearing in the forest, in the middle of which was a jumble of lumber, shingles and half-timbered facades, clearly the remains of an old house. There were no signposts, gates or fences to warn that this was private property. The "intruder" could also have come upon a middle-aged woman, dressed in khaki-coloured work slacks and runners that had seen better days, perhaps with a well-worn Siwash sweater to ward off the chill from an early autumn frost. She might have been bent over picking up scraps of wood intended for stoking the small woodstove in her kitchen. She would seem to be a rather serious woman who had spent a lot of time outdoors.

There were tales of an eccentric and reclusive woman who lived on the property on Curteis Point in the district of North Saanich on Vancouver Island. The muddle of wood and debris was all that was left of her beloved home, which she had called "Little House." The woman, who appeared to say, "Do not interrupt my privacy," was

Capi Blanchet. She has taken thousands of readers cruising up and down the coastal waters of British Columbia with her five children and her dog on a smallish, lightly built boat, through the 1920s and 30s. People have been captivated and charmed by the stories that she so enticingly narrated in her books, *The Curve of Time* and *A Whale Named Henry*, the latter the tale of a little whale who got trapped behind the fearsome rapids in Skookumchuck Narrows.[1]

While Capi wrote a great deal about the magnificent scenery of the British Columbia coastline and the demands of coastal cruising, showing an indomitable spirit, she modestly wrote little of herself. She exists as a shadowy protagonist against the backdrop of her stories; she is there and yet she is not. Who was this woman who shared twelve years of her life in her books? Whatever became of her, what of her children, how did she cope with the vicissitudes of life? With the telling of her story Capi invited readers in, as companions, and in the process created a connection between herself and her audience. She was practical in the assessment of her purpose. Her intention, she wrote, is that *The Curve of Time* "is neither a story nor a log; it is just an account of many long sunny summer months, during many years when the children were young and old enough to take on camping holidays up the coast of British Columbia."[2]

Capi Blanchet, her children—Elizabeth, Frances, Peter, Joan and David—and Pam, the Gordon Setter, were introduced in *The Curve of Time*.[3] First published in 1961 by William Blackwood & Sons of Edinburgh, in Canada in 1968 by Gray's Publishing and more recently by Whitecap Books, *The Curve of Time* is currently in its eleventh printing. It has been on the market for forty-six years, a remarkable achievement when the average shelf life of a book is not much more than three months.

Reviewers and critics alike give high praise to her book. "This book made me want to buy a boat and go on this trip," or "I have gifted this book many

Facing page: L to R: Frances, Peter, Elizabeth, David, Joan, Capi, 1931.

COURTESY JANET BLANCHET

times . . . This is a volume which sticks with you from the day you read it," are typical comments from her readers.[4, 5] It has become a Canadian classic read by thousands of people and is one of the leading books on cruising the Inside Passage from the southeast coast of Vancouver Island to Cape Caution on the mainland coast. The Vancouver Maritime Museum lists it as one of the top 35 maritime books written about British Columbia.

The Curve of Time began as a series of four articles written for *Blackwood's Magazine*, a prestigious periodical that was published in Edinburgh from 1817 to 1980. *Blackwood's Magazine*, more commonly known by its shorter name, *Maga*, had a devoted readership, particularly among British colonials. The magazine often published tales from provincial outposts; readers loved the accounts of pioneering adventures and stories of the sea. Its writers represent an impressive cast of luminaries in the literary world: by-lines like Shelley, Coleridge, George Eliot and Joseph Conrad often graced the pages of *Maga*. Even when its readership was waning in the 1960s, it was still a desirable magazine for a writer to be published in, especially a first-time writer. *Maga* was a magazine that Capi was familiar with and enjoyed. She was also reported to have had an article on her coastal experiences published in *The Atlantic*, another impressive literary and cultural journal with a long history.[6] *The Atlantic*, like *Blackwood's*, was among her regular reading fare; she liked the intellectual and critical capacity that many of the articles demanded, sometimes sharing them with people she met on her coastal cruises.

Capi sent the manuscript of *The Curve of Time* to Blackwood's, the book-publishing arm of Blackwood & Sons, but it proved to be a poor choice. They accepted her manuscript and sent off a contract for her to sign. When Capi received it she was quite excited but, having little experience in such matters, she took it down the lane to have Gray Campbell look it over. Gray was not only a friend but also a writer, who had had a memoir of his ranching life in the foothills of Alberta published. He loved her book and, with enthusiastic ideas about signing parties, book tours and radio interviews, he offered to act as her agent and handle all the publicity. As heady as it all sounded, Capi calmed everyone's enthusiasm. She said to Gray's wife, Eleanor, "He isn't serious, is he? If he is, you must stop him."[7]

Her book went to press in 1961. She received six copies and then

Facing page: Harry Mountain's house, Gwa'yasdams. PHOTO BY CAPI BLANCHET, COURTESY JANET BLANCHET

heard nothing from Blackwood's. Capi eventually wrote to them to find out what had happened and what their intentions were. It seems that they failed to recognize the gem they had. They put out a small print run and made less-than-passing efforts to publicize it: a death-knell for any book. There were no signing parties or interviews of any sort. It was as if her book had never been written. Blackwood's did send seven hundred copies to Toronto but, astonishingly, none to British Columbia. Capi made a loan to a bookstore in Sidney so they could purchase copies from Toronto.[8] Gray acted as an informal marketing manager and sent off reviews of her book to one of Canada's leading historical publications, *The Beaver*. He also contacted CBC Radio, which publicized the book.

Despite the initial setback with Blackwood's, Capi took pleasure in her writing and enjoyed the letters and comments she received in response. Her book has drawn many to discover for themselves the place where Pam the dog stood up to her neck in the ocean all night to escape a cougar, or the location of the homestead of Phil Lavine, an old Frenchman who lived in Laura Cove, or the fog-shrouded villages of the 'Nakwaxda'xw of Ba'a's (Blunden Harbour), the Kwikwasutinexw of Gwa'yasdams (Gilford Village) or the Ławitsis from Kalugwis.[9] Perhaps *The Curve of Time* served as a record for her children, honouring their participation and their contributions to the success of those voyages.

The libraries of many cruising boats on the west coast have a spot reserved just for Capi's book; countless numbers of cruisers have become devotees, recommending it to their friends or passing it from boat to boat. It is easy to get a conversation going with boaters over a dockside meal or chatting in anchorages, teasing out the exact location of many of her adventures. Sometimes charts come out and opinions are offered on where she was and when. Her descriptions are vivid and she was careful, and mostly correct, in the names of the islands, bluffs, inlets, coves and anchorages she visited, but some accounts are vague and obscure; though the mysteries this poses were not intentional, they lead to a puzzlers' delight—boaters love the ambiguity. For example, where exactly did she tow the *Caprice* when the engine quit near the headland at Bullock Bluff?[10]

A quick look at the chart shows Bullock Bluff is at the north end of Cortes Island in Desolation Sound. She probably rowed down Sutil Channel, because the closest anchorage down Lewis Channel, the alternative route, would have been too far for her to row—but she did not say. Her readers are lured on by her reporting that she rowed seven miles to where, in the light of the early morning, she noticed a saltwater fall at the head of the inlet.[11] There are several coves on the chart, as well as many cliffs, and Capi's distance was out, but she most likely took refuge in Von Donop Inlet, on the northwest corner of Cortes Island. She could not have found a more sheltered and peaceful place to spend the day working on her engine.

Facing page: Bullock Bluff.

Sadly, Capi did not live to see the success of her book; she died just six months after its publication. Her footprint on Earth was muted and her nature so unassuming that she probably would have been surprised by its popularity, as well as by the number of articles that have appeared about her.

CHAPTER ONE ⊹

Capi's Early Life

Capi's original name was Muriel Wylie Liffiton. To her children, however, she was just Capi—a nickname that she acquired when she became captain of her own boat, the *Caprice*. She hated the name Muriel and certainly never used it except for formal and legal documents. Even for her by-line she substituted M. Wylie Blanchet, or M. L. Blanchet for Muriel. Capi's middle name, Wylie, stemmed from a family tradition of incorporating ancestral names into their own. Wylie was the maiden name of Capi's maternal great-grandmother, Margaret Wylie of Dumfriesshire, Scotland. Wylie was also the middle name given to her maternal uncle, Harold Wylie Snetsinger.

Capi was raised along the banks of the St. Lawrence River; she spent her childhood exploring the shoreline and tidal flats along the Lachine Canal and the woods and beaches of her grandfather's summer home in Cacouna, Quebec. She was born in Montreal on May 2, 1891, into a loving and close-knit family. She had two sisters: Violet, who was born four years before Capi, and Doris, five years after. Two other children were born to her parents, Charles Albert Liffiton and Carrie Jane (née Snetsinger) Liffiton: Marguerite, their

Facing page: Back row, L to R: Alan Snetsinger, Carrie Jane Snetsinger Liffiton (Capi's mother), Charles Liffiton (Capi's father), Frank Snetsinger. Front row, L to R: Arthur, Edith, Minnie and Harry Snetsinger, 1885. COURTESY ROSEMARY A. JOY

first child, died in infancy and Gray, the only son, died of a fever at seventeen months, when Capi was four.

When Gray became ill with a fever in the summer of 1895, his young body had trouble coping. While the exact nature of his illness is not known, scarlet fever was common among children in Montreal at the time. As his fever intensified and he became more fretful, the doctor was called in but the child died on Friday, July 12. Capi's maternal grandfather, John Gray Goodall Snetsinger, for whom Gray was named, came to his daughter's side as soon as he received word via telegram. Some understanding of events as they transpired is provided through a letter Capi's grandfather wrote to his son Alan, the day after Gray died.

> Saturday July 13/95 [1895]
> Dear Al,
> I had decided to come home all week but had a Telegram from Liffiton saying Gray was very Sick. We then had one last evening saying he was dying and that Charley [Capi's father] was on the way down so I took a morning train and met Charley at Cacouna Station and went down to Metis but the dear child was dead before we got their [sic] I fully expected it. Carrie and Charley with all the children will leave here tomorrow morning. I will meet the children at Cacouna and they will go through the train here on Sunday morning. I'll go through to Montreal tomorrow . . . You could have come down to the funeral but Carrie said there was no use in bringing him down they will bury him on Sunday

morning. Mrs. Bender and all the Visitors here did
all they could for Carrie—there is a Dr. resident here
he did all he could.

From office

Father[1]

The little boy was taken back to be buried in the Cimetiére Mont-Royal in Outremont, next to his baby sister.

Lachine, Quebec, where Capi grew up, was in 1891 a small but burgeoning town. Lachine is on the Île de Montréal, sandwiched between Dorval to the west and Montreal to the east. A close locator point is the Université Concordia–Loyola, which is a seven-minute drive from Capi's old house at 620 Boulevard St. Joseph. It was a melon field in Capi's time but is now a significant university. On its western side, Lachine is bordered by Lac St. Louis and the Lachine Rapids. It is a community rich in history. Originally a farming community, Lachine was settled in 1675 by French immigrants. Later, it was a centre for the fur traders, and one of the houses that Capi and her family lived in was reportedly part of an old Hudson's Bay post. The land surrounding Capi's home was also part of the site of a vigorous contest between the Iroquois Confederacy and the French colonists in the late 1600s.

For Capi's family, living in Lachine provided ready access to one of the largest Canadian ports and the emergent industrialism of the 1880s. When the Lachine Canal was built in 1825 to bypass the turbulent Lachine Rapids, ships could travel safely into the Great Lakes, and they did, up to 15,000 ships a year. Business exploded and set Lachine up to become a core industrial area and an important component of Montreal's expanding economic development. Many businesses grouped themselves around the Saint-Gabriel sector of the canal because of the proximity of hydraulic power; there were cotton mills, flourmills and sugar mills, as well as sawmills, rolling-stock railway factories, tool factories and foundries. It was here that Capi's father located his import-export business.

Charles Liffiton started his working life as a clerk and travelling salesman and by 1879, he had established a partnership known as Bourgeau, Liffiton & Company. They imported coffee, spices and mustard. Coffee, in particular, was rapidly becoming a sought-after item as people's taste for the dark-roasted bean was growing. Charles was apparently successful in import-export and six years after he began his partnership, he became the manager of Acme Mills, also importers of coffee and spices. Why Charles gave up his own company to become the manager of another is unknown. The owner of Acme Mills was John Gray Goodall Snetsinger, a wealthy businessman from Cornwall, Ontario. Charles was energetic and had the experience and the international contacts necessary to build Acme Mills. Being the manager offered more than merely a job for Charles: Snetsinger had a daughter named Carrie Jane, the second child of seven and Snetsinger's first daughter. She and her father were very close and remained so throughout their lives. Charles became enamoured of the petite and fashionable Carrie and eventually asked Snetsinger for his daughter's hand in marriage. The proposal was accepted and wedding arrangements were made.

Facing page: Capi's grandparents, John Gray Goodall Snetsinger and Margaret Irving, on their wedding day, September 13, 1859, in Cornwall, Ontario. COURTESY ROSEMARY A. JOY

On Wednesday, September 16, 1885, Carrie walked through the portals of Trinity Anglican Church in Cornwall, on the arm of her father, to exchange marriage vows with her fiancé.

After the wedding Carrie and her new husband moved to Montreal and took up residence on Lincoln Drive, a little west of Dorval and about seventeen kilometres from where Capi was eventually born. By that time, 1891, Charles was the owner and proprietor of his own firm, C. A. Liffiton & Company. Charles Liffiton was identified in the Montreal City Directory for 1899–1900 as the proprietor of the Acme Coffee and Spice Steam Mills located at 126 and 128 Queen Street. It is not known if Charles bought Acme Mills from his father-in-law or if it was given to him, but Snetsinger no longer appeared in the record as owner. At the time, Acme had some lucrative contracts, being the sole agent in Canada for Macurquhart's of London, dealing with wholesale coffee and spices, Worcestershire sauce, Heinrichs' Refined Family Gelatine and Portland cement, among other items. Charles travelled internationally for his company but it was apparently difficult for smaller companies to succeed; his business faltered and he had to declare bankruptcy in 1900.[2]

This must have had an effect on the family, but they did not seem to suffer from any form of want. Capi's mother, Carrie, was always smartly dressed and photographs of the family show them all in stylish clothing that suggested a comfortable lifestyle. Also, many of their portraits were taken by William Notman, who was the society photographer of upper-class Montreal. Carrie's family was wealthy and letters hint that her father helped them out from time to time. Charles did not give up on owning and operating his own company. Bankruptcies were common in the early 1900s, but they never stopped committed businessmen from starting afresh.

According to the Montreal City Directory for 1901, Liffiton & Company, located at 147 St. James, become involved in real estate, mortgage loans, valuations and fire insurance. Charles was probably still engaged in the importing and exporting business, as he was often away from home for long periods of time, sometimes up to a year.

He wrote regularly to his children when he was away—he called them his "little pets" and they called him Papa. The children were never told where their father was travelling, and he never talked of his work to them. When he arrived home after a business trip, Capi and her sisters would try to find out where he had been by involving him in their geography lessons. They would look at an atlas and point out various countries, asking their father about them, and he would occasionally let slip that he had been to Cairo, Alexandria or other cities in Africa. Even when their father was close

to home, he made sure he connected with his children. A touching letter he wrote to Violet when he was away for only a few days at a regatta at Ste-Anne-de-Bellevue—between Lac St. Louis and Lac des Deux-Montagnes on the western tip of the Île de Montréal—shows his love for his children.

> To Papa's Darling
> Little Violet,
>
> No doubt you will be surprised at getting a Love letter all to yourself as you are still so young. But Papa thought as you had cut some of your first Wisdom teeth that you would appreciate one all to yourself and so I am writing this large and plain so that you may pick it out yourself. No doubt if you find any difficulty Mama will help you . . . and now I will tell you how I had to spin around to drown my lonesomeness for my Little Pets. On Saturday I took the train to Lachine at 1:30 and at Lachine found Major Cole, of course you know the Great Big soldier Major Cole with his Steam Yacht waiting for your Papa. Col Turnbull, Lieutenants Anderson Hostya and Capts

Finlayson and others, 8 in all, and steamed at once for St. Ann's to see the Regatta. It was a lovely trip past Dorval . . . We were late in getting up but saw the . . . Race & several others afterwards. Motored to Rouskin for Super . . . such a crowd . . . got no Potatoes as they were all done had to eat bread with our Roast Beef and Lamb. Could not tell which it was got an ear of corn, also something they called Tapicoa [sic] pudding. Never saw either. We started from St. Ann after nine beautiful moonlight nights. Got to Lachine in time to get the 12 PM train for Home & was in bed by 12:30 and slept until 9:00. It's now late and as papa feels tired he will say good night Darling and Kiss Papa and give one to Mama from your Loving Papa.[3]

Charles loved sports and was known around Montreal as a good yachtsman and a man who excelled at winter sports. It is almost certain that Capi spent summers sailing with her father on the St. Lawrence River. Their father's enthusiasm for outdoor activities had a positive effect on the children. While they enjoyed music and seeing the latest play starring Sarah Bernhardt, their summers were mostly taken up with swimming, tennis, boating and exploring.

Capi considered herself a tomboy; she loved climbing trees and observing the squirrels and the mice that scampered about. Sometimes she brought her finds home with her, hiding them in her pockets and then frightening their tutor when her treasures escaped and scuttled across the classroom floor. She spent hours on the St. Lawrence, watching the various flatfish floating in and out with the tide. She noticed that when the tide was low, they would bury themselves in the sandy flats, with only their eyes peeking out. Sometimes, when she accidentally stepped on one it would wiggle under her feet, making its presence instantly known. This led her to develop a particularly successful technique for catching them, waiting for ". . . a mysterious little tickle under the arch. If you stooped quickly and put a hand on each side of your arch—then you would pull out a little browny-grey flounder. The harpoon men would call out, 'not fair,' but one by one they would all change to 'feet.'"[4] What Capi did not know was that "flounder tramping" was an age-old technique that had been used in the estuaries of southwest Scotland for centuries; in fact, every year in late July the World Flounder Tramping competition is held on the Glen Isle peninsula, south of Palnackie in Scotland.

Violet, Capi's older sister, was an avid tennis player and swimmer. In a postcard she wrote to her father on July 13, 1914, from Cornwall, Ontario, she wrote of her sports activities: "Dear Father: I have played three sets of tennis. It is very hot so will enjoy my swim this afternoon. Uncle Willie's boat has not come yet but we rent the old one." When she could not get out on the court and play a set of tennis, she lamented the fact. In a letter to her mother while she was visiting Paris and London with her aunt Edith Snetsinger, she wrote not only of the wonders of her travels but of also missing tennis.

London, May 20, 1917
My dear Mother:
 Aunt Edith & I are resting today after our journey yesterday. We left Paris at Eight o'clock and did not arrive until eight P.M. . . . We have come back

to cold . . . London. Lachine must be very warm. I
think the idea of a tennis league is a splendid idea. I
do not believe I shall play much tennis here for I long
for a game. Now that the summer is coming I miss
the water of the country . . . We [enjoyed] splendid
operas in Paris . . . Aunt Edith bought two lovely hats
in Paris at Hilsboyers, a very expensive place their
hats are from $50 up. One morning when we were in
bed a girl came up to show us lingerie dresses from a
French house. There they were perfectly beautiful all
hand made the cheapest $40 . . . I am going to buy a
lingerie one in London. I shall find a machine made
one. I cannot pay for hand work.[5]

Capi's family was profoundly religious and the bible held a place
of honour in their home. In fact, Capi's sister, Doris, was so keen on
biblical stories that her father had to read passages from a favourite
volume to her at bedtime for an entire year. Capi was not outwardly
religious, but she was well versed in philosophy and in classical and
religious thought.

On one of her cruising trips up the coast of British Columbia,
Capi lent a book by an Indian mystic to Mike (Andrew Shuttler),
a homesteader in Melanie Cove. She knew Mike did not hold with
religion, but he did like to read and he loved a good argument. She
said nothing when she first handed it to him, wanting to hear his
reaction unfettered by her comments. After he finished he was a
little hesitant about offering his opinion, as he thought Capi might
have liked the book, but then he said it was "Just so much dope. All
words—not how to think or how to live, but how to get things with

no effort!"[6] Capi said she didn't think anyone could have summarized the thoughts presented in the book any better.

As a child, Capi attended church with her family, but her mind wandered on to other things. The low, liquid whistles of the thrushes or the sharp chip of the eastern phoebes as they twittered about in the grass around the quaint wooden church held more interest for her than did the lessons of the sermons. In *The Curve of Time* she reminisced about attending church at Cacouna, most likely St. James of the Apostle, a charming, Romanesque-style building constructed in 1865. "On Sunday mornings," she wrote, "all through the church service in the little white church in the middle of the pine woods—a little church that smelt of scrubbed pine and had hard pine benches to sit on . . . I listened to the thrushes . . . and never heard the service at all."[7]

Doris continued to be very devout and although the family was Anglican, she eventually took up the calling of a Roman Catholic nun. The route to her vocation was circuitous, however. When Doris was twenty-five, she was engaged, and before her marriage she attended a course of religious studies at the Convent of the Sacred Heart. She had been attracted to the Catholic Church for some time and was so taken with the dogma, morals and discipline of Catholicism that she called off her engagement and then, with the fervent devotion borne of her convictions, stepped beyond the bonds of her family and friends and entered the Order of the Society of the Sacred Heart of Jesus. On December 12, 1922, her twenty-sixth birthday, Doris proclaimed her vows. Her family was shocked and none of her relatives attended the ceremony. As difficult as that must have been for her, for she did mention it, Sister Liffiton went on to have a distinguished career, eventually becoming Mother Superior of the order.[8]

Capi never lost contact with Doris, and when Sister Liffiton was assigned to Vancouver from Montreal, to teach at the Sacred Heart Academy in Point Grey, Capi sent her two oldest daughters, Elizabeth and Frances, to school there for two years. Capi occasionally took the ferry from Vancouver Island to see Doris, and she often took her youngest son David, who, like all six-year-olds, had a curiosity that sometimes led him into trouble. On one visit David went exploring the convent on his own and ended up in the nuns' quarters, where no male was allowed. This caused an upset and he quickly learned the consequences of his behaviour. It was something he did not do again and the memory of the incident stuck with him throughout his life.[9]

Capi came from an educated household that encouraged intellectual pursuits. Her mother had been schooled at Mount St. Mary's Convent in Montreal and all three of her daughters were serious readers who enjoyed discussing philosophical ideas. They were initially home-schooled by a hired tutor, as was the custom among the wealthy, and when Capi was fourteen they were sent to St. Paul's Academy. This was a private school run by the Reverend Robert Newton and his wife, at the corner of Sherbrooke Street and Greene Avenue in Westmount, Montreal, not far from their house in Lachine; the daily commute probably took no more than thirty minutes.

When the Liffiton girls attended St. Paul's, it was quite a new school. Established in 1898, it had been open for only seven years. The school was comfortable and had the ambience of a home. At St. Paul's they received a classical education, studying history, literature, Latin and French. All three girls excelled at school, and Capi and Violet competed with each other for top honours. Capi had set her sights set on winning the coveted red-leather-bound Temple volumes of Shakespeare. There were nine volumes in all, given for English, Latin, French, spelling, astronomy, history, geography, geometry and algebra. Capi captured the entire set and was also awarded a special prize of *Antony and Cleopatra* for being the top student in "all subjects."

With such outstanding scholarship, Capi was expected to go on to university, but she chose marriage instead. It was Doris who went on to post-secondary studies, attending both Oxford University in England and the University of Rome.[10] Violet travelled throughout Europe, taking in as much ballet and opera as she could; in 1924 she married a banker, Kenneth Winans, and became a patron of the arts, supporting unknown artists by buying their paintings. Years later Capi said that had she gone on to university she would have liked to study archaeology. Referring to her coastal experiences at a later point in her life, she said, "Perhaps, in a way that is what I did."[11]

Music was also an important element in the family. Music training for the middle and upper classes was deemed an essential part of education for young women, particularly in Montreal. Consequently, music-study programs flourished, and Lachine not only had an examining board awarding diplomas, but its music programs became a model for others to emulate. All three of the girls played the piano, but Doris was particularly talented; she formed a small musical ensemble that gave concerts for friends and family. In later life, Capi's most valuable possession was her Chickering piano, the pre-World War II choice for concerts. She also kept a violin that her grandfather had given her in her youth and played second violin in a small group at Deep Cove near her home in British Columbia. Her at-home practice sessions on the violin were reportedly not easy on the ear and required tact from those who might otherwise comment. According to her family, Capi was generally not open to criticism from others on any matter, and particularly not on her string virtuosity.

Capi's maternal grandfather, John Gray Goodall Snetsinger, was a significant figure in the Liffiton household and very much a part of Capi's early life. He was a successful businessman and politician whose name survives to this day in Ontario: Snetsinger Island, near the Mille Roches Campsite on the Long Sault Parkway section of the St. Lawrence River in Ontario, is just one of the memorials in his honour. His business interests were diverse and profitable. He owned a general store and gristmill, and a large wood yard and sawmill in Moulinette, Ontario, fourteen kilometres west of Cornwall. The general store continued to operate until Moulinette was flooded as part of the hydro and seaway projects of the 1950s. He was the major supplier of fuel for steamers on the Cornwall Canal and traded on the London, New York and Montreal Stock Exchanges. In 1879 he established a branch of his Moulinette business in Cornwall, Ontario, buying the old stone store opposite Rossmore House, one of the most popular hotels between Montreal and Toronto. They carried tobacco, dry goods and ladies' ready-to-wear clothing, and had one of the most extensive stocks in eastern Ontario. In 1883 he built the Snetsinger Block, a large commercial structure on the southwest corner of First and Pitt streets, significant because it housed the Cornwall Commercial College, which became noted for its excellence in training both women and men for careers in commerce.

Facing page: John Gray Goodall Snetsinger. COURTESY ROSEMARY A. JOY

As Capi's grandfather prospered he built a large and beautiful home in Moulinette for his wife, Margaret, (née) Irving and their seven children. He referred to his residence as the "White House," and it was a home that Capi knew well; she spent quite a bit of time there as a child. John Snetsinger was a self-made man of United Empire Loyalist stock who enjoyed his position and all of the social activities that were offered to a man of his status. He travelled extensively abroad. He was a generous man, staunchly religious, and had a strong social consciousness—his

community was well acquainted with his philanthropy. In 1902 Snetsinger donated a chancel, sanctuary and five memorial windows to the picturesque Christ Anglican Church in Moulinette. Because it was such a significant part of Moulinette for over a hundred years, Christ Church was saved from the inundation resulting from the St. Lawrence Power Project, which, in 1958, flooded a thirty-three-mile stretch from Cardinal, Ontario, to Cornwall. Today, Christ Church, restored, stands on a grassy knoll in Upper Canada Village in Ontario, a testament to the dispossessed of Moulinette.

An interest in public affairs saw John Snetsinger through a number of political positions. A staunch Liberal who became a popular politician, he was Warden for Stormont County and succeeded the Honourable John Sanfield Macdonald as member for Cornwall and Stormont County in the Ontario Provincial House. He served in the

provincial house from 1871 to 1879 and in 1896 was elected to the federal House of Commons, where he served in the first Laurier government. He died in 1909 at seventy-six and was interred in Moulinette next to his wife, who had predeceased him by thirty years. When the village was lost to the inundation, the cemetery was moved and both of Capi's grandparents were reburied in the John G. Snetsinger plot in the St. Lawrence Valley Union Cemetery. When Capi's mother, Carrie, died, she was buried alongside her parents and not her husband.

This page: The White House, Moulinette, Ontario, built by John Gray Goodall Snetsinger ca. 1875.

COURTESY ROSEMARY A. JOY

Capi spent her summers at her grandfather's house in Cacouna, a wealthy preserve of Anglophones from Montreal. It is a lovely little village that sits along the southern shore of the lower St. Lawrence River—the Bas-Saint-Laurent region of Quebec. Cacouna is about 456 kilometres from Lachine, a long and tiring trip for the family. It

could be reached by boat, but Capi and her family usually travelled on a train, which ambled along at a slow thirty kilometres an hour. The whole of the Bas-Saint-Laurent region was a very popular destination for tourists. Capi and her family spent some time at Little Métis, a further 156 kilometres east of Cacouna; Little Métis was an old local name for Métis-sur-Mer. Cacouna, however, was their favourite place.

Capi wrote fondly of her summers there. Once, when she and her children were exploring the beach at Storm Bay on the west coast, they came across an old barrel filled with water that smelled of wet barrel staves and moss. Her children were musing over a small lizard in the bottom of the barrel

This page: The Snetsinger family at the White House for the wedding of Edith Snetsinger to Paul Putmann, October 3, 1896. Capi is the little girl at the front left; her father, Charles Liffiton, is standing on the far left; her mother, Carrie Jane Liffiton, is behind and to the right of the woman in the polka-dot scarf. COURTESY TOM LIFFITON

and the incident took Capi back to a time when she was a little girl in Cacouna. There was a similar barrel that smelled the same, and it, too, was filled with cool water. She wrote that whenever she passed it on her way down to the beach, she would raise herself up onto the tips of her toes to drink the water that spilled from the edge. She told her children that when she looked down into the bottom, there was almost always a little lizard sitting there. "Some day, when you are big," she told them, "you will find another barrel with a smell just like this—and a lizard—and it will bring you right back to Storm Bay."[12]

It was said that during the summer months the population of Cacouna doubled. The *Buletin politique* for June 23, 1887, heralded the beginning of the summer with a front-page article that said, "Cacouna, these days, gives the impression of being invaded from all sides: trains, boats and streets are full of strangers who are coming to stay for part or the whole summer season in our location . . . our habitants vacated their large house in order to rent it to tourists . . . 'Sir Lord and Family of the high society.'"[13]

The air in Cacouna was sweet and fresh and the weather cooler than the summer heat of Montreal. Sailboats graced the harbour, and people could enjoy the beaches, take cruises, go bowling or to horse-races, play tennis or golf, or attend one of the many evening galas.

The streets were bordered by leafy-green trees that stretched over wooden sidewalks, offering a rustic ambience for the tourists. The architecture was impressive; there were grand wooden hotels and large Victorian summer homes faced with wide pine boards or clapboard, painted white, blue or red. The Molsons, Canada's brewing family, had a summer house there as did Sir Montague Allan of Allan Ocean Liners; there were sawmill barons and senators. The Snetsinger Villa was a neo-Tudor confection of delights. The gabled roof, ornamental trim on the windows and the large sweeping veranda made the house inviting. It was built in 1854 and purchased in 1876 by Capi's grandfather;[14] the Snetsinger family continued to vacation there for nearly a century. It has stood the test of time, and today it sports an attractive coat of yellow paint accented by white trim. Its carefully tended grounds radiate peacefulness and harmony, uniting its past with the present.

It was in Cacouna that Capi explored and honed her skills as an observer of the natural world, and this would set the tone and direction of her life in British Columbia. She spent hours on the salt marshes watching egrets, herons, plovers or spotted sandpipers working the water's edge, as rotund grey seals basked on the rocks in the estuary. There are 300 species of birds and over 800 species of invertebrates, along with 80 species of fish and 14 kinds of marine mammals that inhabit the lower St. Lawrence.[15] It was a cornucopia of wildlife for Capi to study. From atop a hill she could see the resident belugas or the migrating minke, blue and fin whales swimming in the distance.

Facing page: Margaret Snetsinger, née Irving. COURTESY ROSEMARY A. JOY

The name "Cacouna" itself speaks to the abundance of its habitat: "Kakoua-Nak" means "the land of the porcupine," and it was given to

this area by the Algonquin because of the large number of porcupines that inhabited the region.

Capi returned to Cacouna over and over again. It became not only a place of many fond memories for her but also a place of refuge. When the 1918 influenza pandemic was rampaging across the country—there were over a thousand deaths a day in Canada—Capi escaped to Cacouna. She was pregnant with Peter at the time and pregnant women were especially vulnerable.

Cacouna is still a popular destination for tourists and is currently listed as one of the "Most Beautiful Villages of Quebec," by l'Association des plus beaux villages du Quebec. This is a designation accorded to authentic heritage villages of exceptional quality and Cacouna is one of thirty-two such villages. In time, however, Cacouna would fade into the background of Capi's memories, to be revisited when a smell or a particular bird call brought her tumbling back through the years to her childhood. After she married and left for the coast of British Columbia, she never again scrambled down the cliff on her way to the river or walked along the sandy beaches of Cacouna; she would explore other shores, learn new geologies and sample the offerings of other flora.

When Capi was a teenager, one of her school friends was Helen Blanchet, a girl from a large family in Ottawa. Although they didn't know it at the time, their lives were on a course that would bind their two families together: it was through Helen that Capi met Geoffrey Blanchet, who would become her husband. The Blanchets loved the outdoors. They had a boat on the Rideau Canal for their summer activities, and they enjoyed snowshoeing and skating on the canal in the winter. They camped and hiked and roamed around the Gatineau Hills with their pristine trails and beautifully forested woodlands of maples, white spruce, birch, white and red oak and pine. The family was a quintessential Canadian blend, encompassing both French and English heritage. Helen's father, Ludger Blanchet, was of French ancestry with roots in Canada as far back as 1666, when the first Blanchet immigrated to the New World; his father was Facing page: The Snetsinger Villa, Cacouna, Quebec. COURTESY VIATEUR BEAULIEU a notary public who became a judge of the Quebec Court of Appeal. Her mother, Mary Amelia Hunton, was the daughter of an English immigrant who had a successful dry-goods business in Ottawa.

In 1867 Ludger moved to Ottawa to work as an accountant in the Post Office Department,[16] and he and Mary were married the following year on January 23rd. His office was in the stately West Block of the Parliament Buildings, an impressive structure that had opened the previous year to house the ever-expanding departments of

the government. Ludger was more than an accountant; he was a man of many talents. Besides being an avid sportsman, he had a distinct artistic flair. When his day was done, he would leave his fiduciary responsibilities behind, gather up his pencils and pens and illustrate sessions of Parliament or cover major events in Ottawa for the newspapers. His talent was passed on to his son, Geoffrey, who loved to work in clay, and further on down the line to Geoffrey and Capi's daughter, Joan, who studied art in Vancouver and New York.

Facing page, top: The Blanchet family, Ottawa, ca. 1890. Geoffrey is in the centre at the front. Bottom: Helen Blanchet and Muriel Liffiton, ca. 1905. COURTESY JANET BLANCHET

Of eleven children in the Blanchet family—six boys and five girls—Geoffrey was the youngest. They appeared to be a happy family of modest means, but there were some religious struggles in the household. At one point Ludger decided to leave the Catholic Church and had all of his children, except Helen, rebaptized as Presbyterians. He eventually repented and went back to Catholicism, but his ambivalence toward religion affected Geoffrey many years later when he found himself in a depressed state and lamented the lack of a religious heritage.

It was Geoffrey Blanchet, dark-haired, sensitive and artistic, who captured Capi's heart. They shared a love of music and of the outdoors; they enjoyed tennis, hiking, canoeing, camping and sailing. They were both highly intelligent people; as Geoffrey's sisters said, "he was near genius."[17] It is unknown how long their courtship lasted, but it would have been a far more orderly process than today, with chaperoned events and family involvement interspersed with outdoor activities and quiet discussions. In any case, Geoffrey fell deeply in

love with Capi and asked her to marry him. Capi accepted, although she later said it was a decision that she would regret.[18]

They were married in Lachine, Quebec, on May 30, sometime between 1910 and 1912. A family photograph of the wedding has both 1911 and 1912 pencilled in on the back, while a family genealogy gives 1910 as the date. Their wedding was a formal event; men were in morning coats and top hats, and the bride wore a simple but elegant satin gown with a fitted bodice and layered lace sleeves. Her long tulle veil, attached to a coronet of orange blossoms, covered her face and her bridal train draped gracefully behind her. Her bridesmaids wore long day-dresses and her flower girl an Edwardian dress with a contrasting satin sash and a large hat. Capi's page was dressed smartly in a suit topped with a large Peter Pan collar. Her mother had a long feather boa that reached to the ground, and all the ladies wore wide-brimmed, decorated hats.

Capi and Geoffrey began their married life in Sherbrooke, Quebec, where Geoffrey was a bank manager for the Bank of Commerce, the predecessor to the Canadian Imperial Bank of Commerce. Four of their five children were born at this time: Elizabeth in 1913, Frances fourteen months later, Joan in 1916 and their first son, Peter, in 1919. At some point the family moved to Toronto as Geoffrey was to work in foreign exchange at the bank's head office. The head of the department, a Mr. Campbell, became Geoffrey's friend and godfather to Joan.

Facing page, top: Geoffrey Blanchet skiing with three of his sisters, ca. 1903. Bottom: Mary Amelia Hunton and Ludger Blanchet, Geoffrey's parents. This page: Helen Blanchet. COURTESY JANET BLANCHET

Facing page, top: Muriel Liffiton and
Geoffrey Blanchet. COURTESY JANET
BLANCHET. Bottom: Geoffrey Orme
Blanchet. COURTESY JANET BLANCHET.
This page, top: The Liffiton-Blanchet
wedding, Lachine, Quebec. COURTESY
ROSEMARY A. JOY. Bottom: Muriel
Liffiton in her wedding dress.

COURTESY JANET BLANCHET

Geoffrey was highly regarded, the family was comfortable and life seemed to be going well. Then Campbell became terminally ill with cancer, and Geoffrey was asked to step in and take over as temporary head of the department, while still maintaining his original duties and workload.

As he was trying to balance the two jobs he discovered that a colleague, who also happened to be a friend of his, was embezzling funds. Geoffrey was torn between his friendship with this individual, his duty to the bank and his responsibility to Campbell; duty, loyalty and integrity all weighed heavily on his mind. No matter which decision he made, there was no escaping the fact that people would be hurt—there was no neat, quick fix. For Geoffrey it was a minefield of emotions and the ordeal proved to be his undoing. He apprised the bank executives of the situation, but the strain and anxiety caught up with him. His health collapsed and he could no longer continue to work. It certainly didn't help that while Geoffrey was attending to the embezzling fiasco, all four of the children were extremely ill with influenza, which added to his stress and worry.

The bank valued Geoffrey's ability and expertise and did not want to lose him; they granted him indefinite leave and provided him with a small disability pension. However, Toronto was an expensive place to live, and although Capi had some income from her grandfather Snetsinger's estate, it was not sufficient. They decided that when Geoffrey was strong enough to travel they would go out west. Arthur Blanchet, one of Geoffrey's brothers, was living in North Vancouver at the time, working at Vancouver City Hall, and Capi's uncle and aunt, Henry and Florence Liffiton, lived in Gray's Harbor, Washington. They would not be entirely on their own. Elizabeth said there were the "usual moaning Minnies" who thought they were foolish to attempt such a trip, but Capi was an independent person, a quality that would both exasperate others and stand her in good stead.[19] She never did return to eastern Canada, although two of her daughters would spend some time with their uncle in Ottawa, and relatives would visit them on Vancouver Island from time to time.

Capi was never materialistic but she did appreciate a good car. Even as family members had to tighten their belts and become more frugal, she always had a smart car sitting in her driveway. In fact, at the time of her death she owned a four-year-old Rambler Custom Cross Country Station Wagon. For their trip west Capi and Geoffrey bought a 1922 Willys-Knight touring car, perfect for their move. Known as the "Baby Overland Special," their Willys-Knight was a fairly expensive vehicle that got twenty miles to the gallon. Advertisements for the company said, "A Willys-Knight engine was never known to wear out."[20] It was an elegant car with a long body, rimmed with a running board that folded into distinctive fenders that protected the spoke wheels. Described by one of the children as a car that "had flapping curtains and a great top that

Facing page: Elizabeth, Joan and Frances Blanchet, ca. 1919, in Lachine, Quebec. COURTESY JANET BLANCHET

folded like an elephant sitting down," it was adapted for sleeping.[21] It was perhaps not the most comfortable sleeping arrangement, but it sufficed. Three-and-a-half-year-old Peter, however, slept cosily in a hammock strung from the roof.

In 1922 the family packed up their furniture and belongings and shipped everything out by freight to British Columbia, planning to do some sightseeing and find a place to live before their possessions arrived. They camped along the way, bedding down in their Willys-Knight in the evenings. There were few eateries along the way, much less overnight accommodations. Cross-country road travel was a challenge in the 1920s, even with a sturdy car, and particularly with children who were then nine, eight, six and three, but it was the sort of challenge that Capi and Geoffrey thrived on. Geoffrey was well enough by then to share in the driving, but a fair amount of the responsibility had to be taken by Capi. The West was not yet "just a car ride away"; a Canadian highway link would not be completed until 1943. To get across the country they had to make several detours down through the United States, specifically around Lake Superior, at the Manitoba and Ontario border and in certain parts of the Rockies. At one point, when they were sleeping in their car along the side of a road in Chicago, the local constable woke them up and told them to move on. Many roads in 1922 were not surfaced and encounters with mud, steep grades, potholes and detours were frequent. Most of the roads through the Rockies were still designed for horse-drawn wagons, not cars.

In June, after the long journey, the Blanchet family found themselves motoring down a long, bumpy road on Curteis Point, on the Saanich Peninsula at the south end of Vancouver Island. It was a quiet place; there was little industry in the area and the nearest town, Sidney, was about seven kilometres away. Today Sidney is only a nine-minute drive from the point but in 1922 that seven kilometres represented the remoteness that the Blanchets were looking for. The population of the districts of North Saanich and Sidney was around two thousand. A sawmill supplied jobs, as did the new automobile ferry that ran to Anacortes, Washington, which could be taken for the fare of forty-two dollars. There was a rabbit-breeding industry and chickens were hot topics among the residents—egg sizes were reported daily in the *Sidney and Islands Review*. And for any enterprising person, the town was desperate for a laundry, so much so that the editor of the newspaper chided its readers for their lack of industry. An editorial in the *Review* stated, "At the present time the weary housewife has no other choice but to send the family wash to Victoria when unable to handle the same. A local laundry would be welcome by many and no doubt well patronized. Come on, you laundrymen!"[22]

The area seemed promising. When the Blanchets reached the end of the road, they came upon a gate with the name "Clovelly" secured to it. The property was quite secluded and well protected from the sea breezes, and it looked to be a lovely place to stop and eat their supper. They climbed down from their faithful Willys-Knight and went over to the gate—it was locked. Clearly this place belonged to someone, but it seemed to be abandoned; it gave the impression of an arboretum gone wild. They ignored the lock, climbed over the gate and set about having their meal. Noticing a very narrow lane that just needed to be explored, they followed it around the base of a cliff and into a clearing where they saw a rustic-looking house standing in a hollow.

The house appeared to be built of logs, since a bark exterior served as the façade; there were roses everywhere—on the paths, on the porch and up the main door—and long garlands of climbing roses draped themselves over the roof, dripping off the eaves like icicles. Capi was immediately captivated. In fact, in her photo album there are more pictures of "Little House," as they called it, than of any other subject. In *The Curve of Time* she wrote enchantingly of discovering what was to become their home. "It was the first time we had ever found a little fairy tale house in the middle of a forest, and we didn't know quite what to do. So we called out, 'Little House, Little House, who lives in Little House?' and nobody answered. 'Well, then,' we said, 'we'll live here ourselves,' and we crept in through the window and settled ourselves in Little House."[23] It seemed just the place for the Blanchets, and it happened to be for sale. There was a lot of land available on the peninsula but housing was difficult to find; this was a case of serendipity.

The house, with its buildings and property, which included 2.9 hectares of land with four hundred metres of waterfront, was for sale for $7,500. Capi's uncle, Alan Snetsinger, loaned them $2,000 for the down payment and they arranged a private mortgage in Victoria for the remaining $5,500. By the time Capi died in 1961 the property was reduced to 2.6 hectares and was appraised at $60,500. Forty-three years later, in 2004, a small portion of the original property, .63 hectares, with a house and 130 metres of waterfront, was on the market for $2,800,000. North Saanich is still semi-rural, with small farms and marinas, and Sidney, with its views of the Olympic and Cascade mountain ranges, has become an attractive and appealing seaside town.

Facing page: Little House.
COURTESY JANET BLANCHET

Little House was a rustic retreat. The siding of the house consisted of mill slabs, very cleverly dressed on the top and edges with bark to give it a country-cottage look. The ground floor contained a vestibule and adjoining coat closet, lavatory, hall, library, dining room, kitchen, scullery, larder and pantry. The second floor had a hall, three bedrooms, two dressing rooms, two bathrooms, a lavatory and a linen closet.

Elsewhere on the property there was a big water tower built in the same style; it was reminiscent of a fort. It had a 3,800-litre water tank on the top floor, a garage on the ground floor and a servant's room on the second level. The original plans referred to this as the "Chinaman's room"; it was 2.6 metres square. The garden had obviously been very beautiful. In fact, when Mr. Moresby-White, the original owner, resided in the house, the grounds had been carefully maintained by a number of Chinese gardeners, who lived in outbuildings behind the main house.

Little House had sat empty for a number of years and re-quired a lot of work. There was dry rot in the foundations. The roof sagged and the cement chinks that filled the gap between the rafters made it too heavy; it was not much good at keeping out the weather either—the

woodpeckers had been at it—so it needed replacing. David, Capi's son, said that he learned all he knew about house building by looking at Little House and seeing how things should not be done. The primary problem was the lack of a foundation; there was nothing to prevent the timbers that rested upon the damp ground from rotting. The structure's main supports were large boulders at each corner, so the whole thing drooped. Despite its appearance, Little House had a very impressive beginning. It had been designed by one of Victoria's most famous architects, Samuel Maclure.

From the 1890s to the 1940s, Maclure influenced much of the

residential architecture in the province and designed some of Victoria's most impressive buildings. While he worked in many styles, including Georgian and Tudor Revival, he created a distinctive West Coast look. He used native materials, combining rustic slabs of bark-covered fir with field-stone masonry or local shingles on the exterior. Clovelly was designed in his rustic style and is very similar to The Latch Inn and Restaurant, now an upscale inn on Harbour Road in Sidney.[24] The Latch, originally called Miraloma, was the summer residence of the Honourable Walter Cameron Nichol, who was the Lieutenant-Governor of BC from 1920 to 1926. Both The Latch and Clovelly balanced the rustic with polished sophistication. Photographs and drawings of Clovelly were put on display at the *Architecture and Allied Arts* exhibit in New York in 1925. The house also garnered international attention when an article in the *Paris Review Moderne* praised the design and described the house as "la maison forestiere."[25]

Years later Capi met Samuel Maclure at a party and mentioned that she lived in a house he had designed. When she described it, Maclure is reported to have said, "Oh yes—one of my more artistic efforts," and then moved away immediately.[26] The house was built in 1915 for A. Moresby-White of whom little is known. It is possible he built it for his bride, Miss Leigh Pemberton, who was the daughter of Sir Edward and Lady Leigh Pemberton of Kent, England.[27] There was a suggestion that Moresby-White was engaged in real estate promotion on Curteis Point, but the collapse of the property boom coupled with the beginning of World War I may have put a stop to any schemes that he had for the property. Moresby-White apparently left the Saanich Peninsula and seems to have dropped out of sight.[28]

When the Blanchets first stepped into the house it had echoes of a once-lively time. The principal bedroom had numerous hooks in the ceiling from which hung the broken remains of coloured Japanese lanterns, a mystery until sometime in the late 1930s when a woman knocked on the front door and asked permission to look around. She said that the thing she most remembered about the house were the magnificent parties that Moresby-White gave.

Facing page: Front elevation of the water tower, designed by Samuel Maclure. COURTESY SPECIAL COLLECTIONS, MCPHERSON LIBRARY, UNIVERSITY OF VICTORIA

Parties in the 1920s were always festive events. There was a passion for things Asian, and crepe, tissue and Japanese lanterns were the preferred party decorations. Women wore long, sensuous, black, gold or coral lamé gowns accented by line-thin rhinestone bracelets. Was this the type of parties given at Clovelly? Years later David found a gold bangle in one of the flowerbeds, perhaps a leftover from a party. For the new owners there would be no grand parties, but children would laugh, squabble, play and be born in this house. Death and great sadness would approach, but it was also from here that grand ventures would unfold. Little House would shelter the Blanchets for twenty-four years until, in 1946, the house finally succumbed to its poor construction and had to be torn down.

Once the Blanchets obtained ownership of their house, life took on a come-what-may style. They had to be careful of their finances, and Capi made it clear to the children that they were now responsible for picking up after themselves, as they would no longer have a maid to help around the house. They raised turkeys and chickens, tended their vegetable garden, fished and beachcombed for wood—always slightly damp—for burning in the stately fireplace that was the centrepiece of the living room. "Money wasn't flowing like honey but there was enough," Elizabeth once remarked.[29] They went on family outings, hiked and swam in the cove by their house. Thousands of kilometres of shoreline, with bays and archipelagos, stretch from Puget Sound to Alaska. It is probably difficult to live, as they did, on a point of land watching fishboats, tugs, freighters and private schooners pass by their doorstep and not succumb to the lure of the ocean. And succumb they did.

Shortly after their arrival the Blanchets begin looking for a boat. They were not in the market to buy the boat of their dreams but thought if they searched hard enough, they would find just the right one. When they found "their" boat it was at Brentwood Bay, not far from their home. It looked a little the worse for wear but the price was right; it was only six hundred dollars, and they bought it on the spot. There was a slight problem, however; the *Caprice* had been sitting on the bottom of Saanich Inlet. It had sunk after the Brentwood Bay ferry hit a chunk of ice, which ricocheted off the *Caprice*. Victoria is well known for its temperate winter climate but the winter of 1923 was a bitter one with a record-breaking snowfall. In one day alone more than fifty centimetres of snow landed on the docks at Brentwood Bay and ice appeared in the inlet.

When Capi and Geoffrey first saw the *Caprice* it must have been quite a sight. Boats have a spirit about them but a boat that has sunk and then been hauled up out of the ocean is bleak and soulless, as if it has been stripped of its very essence. It is not known how long the boat sat on the bottom of the inlet, but it had not been long out of the water when the Blanchets found it. Water was seeping out its seams and the engine was encrusted in salt. But it appeared to be a plucky little boat and with the right amount of care, they reckoned, it could surely be put back into service. Capi set to work immediately. She was not terribly domestic, although she could cook a good meal, but she was quite mechanically minded.

The *Caprice* had a Kermath four-cylinder gasoline engine that was popular in the 1920s. The structure of the vessel could be attended to, but seawater is hard on boat engines. The salt particles deposited on an engine that has been submerged are hygroscopic and extract moisture from the air. The result is a thin film of brine on the engine and significantly increased corrosion. The most vulnerable parts of an engine are the internal sections that are difficult to get to. Capi had to

soak the engine in an inhibitive solution such as oil, kerosene or water before she took it apart. Keeping the pH level just right to avoid further corrosion is a chore and demands constant monitoring. She carefully cleaned out all the parts of the engine, brushing, scraping and chipping at any corroded bits. She ground the valves, changed the rings, put in a new magneto ignition system, changed the spark plugs and added new wiring.[30] As Capi and Geoffrey worked on the engine, tensions built up. Elizabeth said that she "did an awful lot of praying that the engine would start."[31] It was very intensive work, and her father, who was usually quite reserved, was doing a goodly amount of swearing. After the engine got a new paint job the *Caprice* was back in business. The motto "A Kermath always runs" was to prove correct for, with regular maintenance, that engine ran for the next twenty-three years.

Facing page: The *Caprice*.
COURTESY JANET BLANCHET

The *Caprice* was a 7.6-metre cabin cruiser built of half-inch cedar planks. It had a vertical bow, typical of the boats of that time, and was sleek, with a beam of only 1.98 metres. There is no additional information on the structure of the boat. The *Caprice* did not seem to belong to any distinct lineage. There were many small-boat builders on the coast at that time, as well as backyard hobbyists, some of whom used plans ordered from magazines. The *Caprice* was typical of boats built in the 1920s, which were referred to simply as gasboats. There was a pilothouse of sorts, a canopy with canvas sides that could be snapped tight to keep out downpours or cold winds. All in all, it was not a particularly sturdy boat and certainly not one likely to take a family of six, plus a dog, through strong tidal currents or threatening weather. Nonetheless, the *Caprice* took its family cruising safely up and down the BC coast for many years.

A lot had happened since Geoffrey had left the employ of the Bank of Commerce, but the hoped-for "cure" had not materialized. He was still dealing with depression. He was not eating much and became very thin, and he could be quite trying at times. In a letter to her brother David, Elizabeth wrote of that time saying that "he must have been very difficult to live with."[32] It probably did not help that Capi and Geoffrey were polar opposites in terms of their personalities. She was a very strong person, determined and focussed on the practical, while Geoffrey was sensitive and melancholic. Capi used to say that Geoffrey was like a delicately jewelled Swiss watch trying to keep pace with the more pedestrian Ingersoll watch.[33]

Capi was pregnant with David, and with so much on her plate she was neither patient nor understanding. Depression was not considered an illness at that time. The medical thinking was that depression was environmental; change the environment and you cure the depression. Geoffrey's sister, Gertie, did arrange for him to see a noted psychiatrist in New York, but his analysis and prescription were Freudian, concerned more with libido than with useful suggestions; Geoffrey was disappointed in the meeting. He later came across a book titled *The Conquest of Fear* that seemed to help him. After reading it he was more optimistic and put on weight, and life in general looked promising.

Everything seemed to be back to normal. Capi was concerned about how to manage during the latter part of her pregnancy, and Geoffrey rose to the occasion. He loved taking care of Capi; he couldn't do enough for her. The children all helped, as well; Elizabeth did the cooking and baked the bread and they all managed beautifully. Capi

wanted to have the baby at home rather than go to the hospital and the doctor agreed, as long as they hired a live-in nurse. John David Hilary Blanchet was born on May 22, 1924, to a very excited family. "Little Dai'd" became their pet name for him. The family was happy, but all was not well with the nurse, and problems arose immediately. She had the air of an army sergeant: things were to run according to her command and she put Capi and her new babe on a round-the-clock feeding schedule. However, this was Capi's fifth child and she knew a thing or two about babies, nursing and the need for sleep. The nurse lasted exactly three days before she was sacked.

Life continued on much as before, and the *Caprice* became an important part of the family's activities. Capi and Geoffrey frequently piled all five children into the boat and took off to explore the nearby islands. There are five major islands and over thirty-nine smaller ones within range of their doorstep: perfect for picnicking, scavenging or picking wild blackberries, rosehips or Oregon grape to be made into delicious jellies and jams. Capi home-schooled her children, so these trips were like labs for their studies. They could examine the many tide pools filled with purple and orange sea stars, all massed together to conserve moisture, or watch the green and white sea anemones as they moved their tentacles in a liquid dance, waiting to capture small crustaceans or tiny marine larvae. They could hone their navigation skills in the relative safety of their "backyard," and witness how weather patterns affected the seas. Boating on the coast was different from what they had been used to, and the Blanchets learned as they went along. Sometimes this ad hoc approach got them into trouble. Once the *Caprice* was stranded high and dry because Capi and Geoffrey didn't believe the tide tables. The tidal range for the Gulf Islands is four metres on a large tide—something they possibly did not take into account.

With Geoffrey on the upswing, his artistic nature blossomed and he ventured into sculpting. He did not have to go far for his materials—there was an ample supply of clay on the property—and the water tower was a perfect place for him to set up his studio. It was high enough that children could not disturb his work, the light was good and it was quiet, allowing him time to concentrate. His daughters did quite a lot of the posing for him, and one of the things he sculpted was an attractive figurine in classical Greek style. Little Dai'd, who had all the natural curiosity of a two-year-old, had been watching his sisters climb up the ladder and disappear into the water tower above and, when no one was watching, he decided that he, too, would climb that ladder and see what was going on.

Up he went, his little legs and hands struggling to reach the widely separated rungs. It was a difficult climb and once he reached the top he had to swing around the side of the ladder to reach a narrow gangway that led into his father's studio. The wonders that lay before him were worth the effort. There was clay to play with and tools to stick into the clay, allowing him to create animals, long rolled snakes, pottery pies and anything else his imagination could conjure up. He was missing for some time. His parents looked everywhere for him and were frantic, fearing the worst. Finally, in desperation, his father thought of the studio. Grateful that his son was safe, Geoffrey scooped him up in his arms and handed him down to his very anxious mother. David was probably too young to be sent to the "naughty mound," which is where the children were told to go when they acted up, but he definitely knew that he had caused a great disturbance that day.

Around this time Geoffrey and Capi began having marital difficulties. Neither was particularly good at communicating their needs to the other, which sometimes led to conflict, hurt feelings and misunderstandings. Despite their differences, Geoffrey was very much in love with Capi but she started to withdraw from him. Adding to this stress and tension were financial problems, five growing children and an interfering neighbour. The children sensed the discord: David became anxious, started vomiting and had nightmares; Joan threw temper tantrums; and Frances refused to eat certain foods. In addition, the girls thought that David and Peter were receiving preferential treatment from their mother. Years later, in a letter Elizabeth wrote to David, she said, "We girls resented the extra attention Tate [Peter] and you got—silly things like arrowroot biscuits—and dish gravy—and bananas—and Eagle Brand Condensed milk—we teased Tate unmercifully and called him Red-nosed-Tate and we did the same to you because we were convinced that Capi only loved sons."[34]

Now Geoffrey's physical health began to decline. He suffered a terrible chill in 1925 when he jumped overboard from the *Caprice* to untangle a rope that had caught around the propeller, and he apparently had a heart attack then. Later in summer he had another one, while they were anchored in Buccaneer Bay, off the Sunshine Coast. There was no medical help nearby, and they were far from home—about one hundred and fifty kilometres, which was a solid fourteen-hour run in good weather. Nothing could be done until they got home. When they arrived back in Sidney, Geoffrey went to Rest Haven, the local hospital, for a check-up. The doctor found that he had some heart lesions, which could have been indicative of a heart attack. Although electrocardiographs were in use in North America as early as 1919, it is doubtful that Geoffrey's doctor had access to such a machine. In fact, very little was known about heart disease at the time, and coronary artery disease, as a cause of death, barely registered on the medical radar. The doctor would have not been able to do much more than listen to his chest through a stethoscope. Unfortunately, most of Geoffrey's health problems were opaque issues in the medical world of the 1920s, and he was primarily left to his own devices for treatment and care. One of the ways he dealt with his latest diagnosis was to keep the doctor's findings to himself—he specifically asked the doctor not to tell his wife.

Geoffrey thought that things might get better if he went back to work; the income would at least help to ease the financial strain. He wrote to the bank, asking to be considered for reinstatement, and in the interim went off to the prairies to look for work on the harvest. This turned out to be a bad decision. The living conditions were appalling and the physical demands of the job were extremely strenuous. Geoffrey was a very fastidious and tidy person, almost obsessively so, his daughter Elizabeth said, and he found the boarding house in which he had to live filthy and completely unacceptable. Also, this once fit and athletic man was simply not up to the work. Geoffrey left his harvest job and found his way to his brother, Guy, who was somewhere in Alberta. Guy had been exploring in the Barren Lands, searching for the source of the Thelon River, and had come out of the north about this time. He sometimes stopped in Edmonton, which may have been where Geoffrey met him. Guy was a mining engineer and Dominion land surveyor of legendary abilities who had mapped over 300,000 square kilometres of the Great Slave Lake area and could out-hike, out-pack and out-paddle most men. He realized that his younger brother was not well and took him back to the coast and to his family.

Upon Geoffrey's return things seemed to improve; temporary rifts were resolved and there was no more arguing. In the autumn of 1926 he needed to follow up on some personal business in Ganges,

on Salt Spring Island, a few miles from Curteis Point. He set out in the *Caprice* on Wednesday, September 9. It was a lovely fall day, with a temperature of 22°C. The sun was shining and there was almost no wind to speak of—SW 2 knots. On the way over he stopped in at Knapp Island, most likely at Trapper Bay, a nice little lunch spot not far from Sidney. He set his anchor and put his meal on the Coleman stove to cook. He then took his watch off, put his clothing aside and dropped the ladder over the side, presumably with the intention of going for a short dip in the ocean. He was never seen or heard from again; he simply disappeared.

The *Caprice* was found abandoned the next day. The Chinese cook who worked for Colonel J.S. Harvey had noticed the boat on Wednesday and thought nothing of it, but when he saw it still anchored in the same spot the following morning, he grew concerned and shouted out to whoever might be in the boat to see if they were all right. It was not uncommon for boats to be moored in the small cove for a day or so, but there was usually activity on deck. When the cook did not get a response, he notified Colonel Harvey's wife. That afternoon Mrs. Harvey rowed out to the *Caprice* and saw that the boat was deserted. She noticed a set of men's clothing on the seat and the small ladder hanging over the side. When she notified the provincial police, constables Jacklin and Thompson were dispatched to the scene. They searched the surrounding area and advised those living along the waterfront, as well as boaters and ships in the vicinity of Sidney and nearby islands, to watch for the missing man.

Despite an area-wide search, Geoffrey's body was never found. The waters around Knapp Island are shallow but the currents are strong and the water quickly drops off to over twenty metres. In all probability Geoffrey was swept out of the protection of the cove. If he had remained in the shallower and warmer water, the searchers might have been able to find him, but in deep, cold water the situation is different. Upon drowning, a victim will sink to the bottom, once the air bubbles from clothing are expelled, and remain there until gas formation creates enough buoyancy to cause a resurfacing. In warm, shallow waters that may take as little as two days, but in water temperatures of 7°C and below, decomposition can take several weeks. If the body is in deep water it may never resurface.

Geoffrey's disappearance was front-page news. The September 11, 1926, edition of the *Daily Colonist* in Victoria said, "The presence of the small ladder over the side is basis for a theory that Blanchet was drowned while taking an early morning swim. Having been informed that the missing man suffered from a weak heart, Provincial Police are inclined to give credence to this explanation of his disappearance."[35] The police had ruled out foul play because nothing was disturbed or had been taken. Geoffrey's watch, along with all the money that was in his coat, was untouched, and his clothing was neatly folded up, lying on the seat. There was no sign of disorder of any kind. They knew that Geoffrey had already had two possible heart attacks while swimming in cold water, and this, along with the food left cooking on the stove, led the police to rule out suicide. Drowning seemed the most likely explanation. The surface water temperature in September would have been around 11°C, which was certainly cold for a man with a weak heart. Any cold-water shock to the body can cause death from drowning due to hypothermia and/or cardiovascular collapse.

There was a great deal of speculation as to what had happened. Was it foul play, suicide or just an unfortunate accident? The disappearance could easily have read like a suicide. Geoffrey was a sensitive, artistic man with a recent history of depression and failing health, and there were tensions in the marriage, so the suicide theory was the subject of much gossip. Even Geoffrey's sister, Gertie, was concerned about a possible suicide and "went snooping about," as Capi said.[36] The children knew nothing of this until they overheard a family friend ask Capi if she thought Geoffrey had committed suicide. It was bad enough to have lost their father but to hear such speculative gossip was devastating.

All these rumours must have been extremely hard for Capi. She was thirty-five years old and now the sole support of her family; her oldest child was fourteen and her youngest just a little over two. One of the ways she dealt with the situation was not to talk to the children about their father's death. In fact, she never talked to anybody about Geoffrey's death. This may have caused some problems for the children. Joan, who was ten at the time, saw her father in her dreams wearing his grey dressing gown and bending over her—he was always worried about her tantrums. Elizabeth dreamed for years of finding her father somewhere, recovering from amnesia, and would sometimes wake up screaming. For a long time she was convinced that her mother was in some way to blame for her father's death. The younger ones did not know that Geoffrey's body had never been recovered and thought that he was buried in the Royal Oak Cemetery near Victoria.[37] The best gift Capi could give them all was to remain level-headed and calm. For their sake she could not allow herself the luxury of grief, but the tug between her feelings and her duties to her children was clearly expressed in *The Curve of Time*. "Death comes to everyone in their time. We who are nearest go with them up the long golden stairs . . . A trumpet shrills—a gate clangs and we are left standing without. Then down the long stairs we retrace our steps to earth . . . numb and

still . . . But small hands are tugging and voices are insistent."[38]

In addition to the emotional trauma of losing her husband, Capi faced bureaucratic hurdles and legal complications in settling Geoffrey's estate. Because he died intestate—that is, without a will, codicil or testamentary papers—she had to obtain custody of the property by applying to the court for letters of administration appointing her the administrator of the estate. The matter was further complicated because there was no body, so no death certificate could be issued.

Capi's family in the east were concerned that she would not be able to manage. They wrote letters and sent telegrams imploring her to come home, saying that it was not good for the children and that she was too young to live in such isolation. They asked that she send a telegram in response. It was all too much for Capi. "How nicely they had my life planned out," she wrote.[39] The estate was not yet settled, but sometime in early October Capi gathered her children around her for a special council. She lit a fire in the big stone fireplace and

read them the letters that the family had sent: "Impossible, impossible . . . impossible," she read, "not fair to the children. Pack up at
once."[40] Tears were shed all around.

    This was an important decision, and, as it would affect all of them,
Capi wanted the children to voice their opinions. She firmly believed
that parents must listen to their children and take their concerns into
account. (There was a time when she had ignored this dictum. She was
having a conversation with someone
when Elizabeth came running up, Facing page: Standing, L to R: Joan,
saying that all of the children were Aunt Gertrude, Peter. In front,
down at the cove. Capi interrupted David and Capi. This page: Uncle
her daughter to remind her of another Arthur, Frances, Joan, early 1930s.
rule, "Children must have an adult COURTESY JANET BLANCHET
with them when they go down to the
sea." Elizabeth, who knew not to interrupt her mother while she was
talking to someone else, waited until she had finished and then said,

"Frances went swimming, and she hasn't come up yet." Without another word, Capi raced to the cove, pulled Frances out of the water and was able to successfully pump the water out of her lungs.[41])

It was not a hard choice for the family; they simply couldn't imagine living anywhere else. Little David was so upset at the thought of moving that he hid in the dog's kennel under the stairs and proclaimed that he was not going to live in the city, he was going to stay right where he had always lived. It was a unanimous decision. They would stay at Little House and continue on as before. Capi telegraphed her relatives the following day and told them that she was staying put. As to their concern that she could not manage on her own, her response was a terse, "Can't I?"

Although Capi remained in contact with both the Liffitons and Blanchets, she never went back east to see them. However, various members of her family did come to visit from time to time. All three of Geoffrey's sisters and two of his brothers visited with Capi and the children at Curteis Point, and when Guy retired, he and his wife, Eileen, moved to Oak Bay in Victoria and saw Capi often. Also, Helen, with whom Capi had gone to school in Montreal, lived with Guy and Eileen in Victoria from about 1940 until her death in the 1960s. As for other members of her family, Capi kept in touch through letters, and though she was not outwardly social, she did have friends who looked out for her. She would not be alone.

After Geoffrey's death, Capi focussed on the children and did not have time for much else in her life. She did not "date," nor was she interested in remarrying. Whenever a strange man came to fix something around the house or do some work on the property, the children would look him over, eyeing him suspiciously, to see if he could pass muster as a possible stepfather. Two years after Geoffrey died, Capi rented Little House to a couple from Washington and set out in the *Caprice* with her children and the dog on what was to become their annual trek up the coast of British Columbia for the next twelve years. The money from the rent would help boost her income, and the cruising would give the family a chance to explore the coast together.

CHAPTER TWO

After Geoffrey's Death—Preparing for Cruising

M. Wylie Blanchet was an exceptional writer; there is a physical eloquence to her writing. Through the sensitivity and insight of her stories she invites readers on a magical voyage during the summers she and her children cruised the coastal waters of British Columbia. She captures the heart, the force, the chi of the coast, as she hovers on *The Curve of Time* where past and future are no more. She presents tantalizing but transient images of place, light and colour.

Her readers journey with her across the wind-swept Strait of Georgia, up through the sheltering waters of the Copeland Islands and into Desolation Sound, exploring inlets, rocky shores, islands and archipelagos. She introduces the many characters who inhabit the bays and coves: the fishermen, the loggers and the settlers. She cruises past "flea village," where Captain Vancouver's men were set upon by swarms of blood-sucking fleas, and walks through a bone-chilling cabin that reeks of death and evil. As she moves farther up the coast, through the turbulent waters of the Yuculta, Dent and Green Point rapids, she slips silently between the misty islets of the Broughton Archipelago, where she is greeted by *dzunuḵwa* (Dsonoqua), a mythical wild woman, a sentinel overlooking Tribune Channel.

Facing page: The *Caprice* taken from the *Ivanhoe*. COURTESY JANET BLANCHET

She visits Gwa'yasdams, Kalugwis and Tsadzis'nukwaame' and bears witness to the many First Nations villages that are proud testaments to a people rich in culture and history. She writes of quietly observing a shaggy grey wolf watching her cubs tumbling on the grass and encounters bears hunting in river estuaries. Then, with trepidation and some concern for a boat not really appropriate for the rigours of the open ocean, she leaves the Broughton and goes out into the Pacific swells of Queen Charlotte Strait, on her way to transit the notorious Nakwakto Rapids; boats have sunk in the uncontrollable whirlpools and standing waves of these waters. And then, almost without warning, when fears are conquered, skills honed, inlets explored and energy expended, she turns toward home.

While her narrative is evocative and enchanting to her readers,

her children did not necessarily agree with her interpretation of their summer trips. When Elizabeth, who became an accomplished writer in her own right, first read her mother's book, she remarked, "A lot of what is in that book is bunk, I ought to know, I was there."[1] Some of the others chose not to read it or did not comment on it. David refused to read the book until he was confined to his bed with polio and his wife read him the chapter about Princess Louisa Inlet. His only comment was, "Well, she got that right," but he never did read the rest.[2] Capi, of course, wrote of the happy times, the discoveries, the thrills, the sunny days. Bad weather and unpleasant disagreements would naturally not find their way into such a book. There were days and sometimes weeks when rain, cold and exhaustion affected them all, when the effort of just surviving was challenging and wearing. Then, too, children have a different perspective from their parents about most things.

Capi was not the first woman to cruise on her own. There were certainly skilled and capable women operating boats on the coast. For some it was a necessity and for others purely recreational. Women who lived in isolated coastal outposts had to know how to operate a boat, because if their husbands became ill or injured they had only themselves to look to for help. Fishermen sometimes took their wives and daughters out with them to run the boat, while they brought in the catch; the women had to learn to manoeuvre the boats through strong currents and bad weather as the fish-laden nets or lines were pulled up. Some women excelled as recreational boaters; harnessing and

Facing page: Kalugwis. The tall pole was carved by Charlie James, Mungo Martin's stepfather. The two facing the water are Thunderbird and human poles. PHOTO BY CAPI BLANCHET, COURTESY JANET BLANCHET

manipulating the wind could be learned by women as easily as by men. The Royal Victoria Yacht Club, the oldest yacht club on the coast, had women racing crews in the late 1890s.

Capi never fell prey to the dictates of cultural norms regarding women and boating. She had been raised around boats, she enjoyed being on the water and probably did not give a thought to what she as a woman should and should not do. Her eldest daughter wrote, "She could do almost anything that men did, and still be feminine."[3] "The first summer they were off in the *Caprice*, men everywhere made a fuss of her—partly because of her shorts—partly because of her capable handling of the boat."[4] Capi had taken the *Caprice* out by herself many times before they started their summer cruising. She was quite competent and determined, but Geoffrey had always been there as a back-up, not that she would probably admit to this. Peter told of the first time she took the *Caprice* out on her own and had a hard time getting the engine to start. "She cranked and cranked that darned engine," he said, "and still it wouldn't start. She could see my father sitting on the Point watching to see if we would get off and she had to go and get him, which really irked her."[5] While confident in her abilities, Capi never overestimated her mechanical skills, and though she was usually calm she could get a bit edgy when the *Caprice* was taking on green water or was at the mercy of the strong currents, swirling back eddies, whirlpools or reversing falls that are common on the coast. With her husband gone, she assumed several important roles: she was skipper, navigator, mother and provider—an onerous responsibility for any single individual. Another issue was that the children were now dependent on just one person to bring them home

Facing page: Capi in the wheelhouse of the *Caprice*. COURTESY JANET BLANCHET

AFTER GEOFFREY'S DEATH—PREPARING FOR CRUISING   69

safely. These were matters, however, that neither Capi nor the children seemed to focus on, or if they did, they rarely expressed concern. Most moments of anxiety were tossed off with one or another saying, "Aren't we sillies," which was meant to comfort.

Every year in early June, the family of six, plus one dog, would pack up their belongings and set off on their summer's adventure. Then, sometime in late September, when there was a nip in the air and the nights began to close in, they returned to the familiarity and comfort of the home that sat waiting for them in the glen by the water's edge. "You just said suddenly, 'We'll probably leave for home tomorrow.' You started off . . . and you arrived . . . You probably decided suddenly because the weather was unexpectedly good for the moment and the glass had steadied. Calm, fine weather the last week in September is like a gift."[6] It was not something to be refused, Capi said.

Facing page: Capi with Pam, the Gordon Setter puppy. COURTESY JANET BLANCHET

Their agenda was as varied as the weather. They were in no hurry, time was languid; it did not matter or perhaps did not even exist. The filament of time is threaded throughout Capi's book. In fact, its very title, *The Curve of Time*, was taken from a book she once read about the relativity of time. Capi was an avid reader and had in her collection of books writings by Count Maurice Polydore-Marie-Bernard Maeterlinck.

Maeterlinck was a compelling and prolific playwright, essayist and poet who won the Nobel Prize for Literature in 1911. He often wrote of mysticism, karma, nature and wisdom as antidotes to materialism, science and mechanization, and the concepts of space and time were the subject of many of his plays. What intrigued Capi was Maeterlinck's suggestion

that time was not merely a succession of irreversible events but existed along a continuum or curve in which past, present and future are all the same. It is our conscious mind, he postulated, that creates these distinctions. The temporality of time was a topic in vogue among artists, writers and intellectuals of the late nineteenth and early twentieth centuries and, while open to differing interpretations, it acted as a stimulus for them to shake off the conventions of linear perspective, expand into non-representational abstractions and create images beyond their normal scope.

Capi artfully used Maeterlinck's notion of time to link her night-time dreams to events that had happened, were happening or might happen. Several times during their travels, in fact, Capi found herself standing on the curve of time—looking both forward and backward. One such event took place in Prince of Wales Reach, a long, narrow stretch of water on the Sunshine Coast. They were on their way to see Chatterbox Falls, farther up in Princess Louisa Inlet, and she decided to stop at Vancouver Bay to have lunch and do a bit of freshwater fishing; trout would be nice for supper, she thought. She left the children playing on the shoreline while she hiked deep into the forest to try her luck at one of the trout streams that she had heard about. Capi was so taken with the beauty and peace of her surroundings that she became lost in what she was doing. Suddenly, she was jolted out of her reverie by a feeling of urgency that struck her with such ferocity that she could not ignore it. An overwhelming and impending sense of doom sent her hurtling back down the path to her children.

"I . . . scrambled through to the beach—blood streaming down my legs, face scratched, hands torn—blood everywhere," she recounted. "Five wondering faces looked at me in horror. The two youngest burst into tears at the sight of this remnant of what had once been their Mummy. 'Are you all right?' I gasped."[7] The children told their mother that there was a strange-looking man down the beach who had been watching them for some time. When he dropped onto all fours and started coming their way, Capi realized it was not a man but a bear. The children, it seems, were between a sow and her cubs. The fish was dropped on the spot and they quickly rowed out to the *Caprice*. Capi had had a dream the previous night that was filled with fear and trepidation and left her with a sense of foreboding. For a moment she had stood on the curve of time as the present and past had come together to warn her that her children were in danger. Being somewhat scientific in her approach to the world and not wanting to give credence to the notion of presentiment or precognition, she argued with herself. "I could have smelt the bear down-wind," she reasoned. "But I knew that the panic and sense of urgency by the

stream, and the feeling in my dream, had been one and the same."[8] The children bemoaned the loss of fish for their supper, but the bear no doubt enjoyed her unexpected gift of food.

Capi referred to their summer expeditions as more camping than cruising. Their boat was small and cramped so they spent much of their time ashore—hiking, fishing, beachcombing, resting and enjoying the welcome warmth of a nighttime campfire. Provisioning the boat for a four-month journey required a great deal of forethought; there was no space for extras. Five children, one dog, one adult, and a summer's worth of dry goods, tools, lines and ropes, cooking utensils, clothing, bedding, charts, books and necessary sundries all needed to fit into a space not much larger than a broom closet. Each person was allowed one outfit that would have to last through all eventualities of weather and conditions. They could also take one pair of pyjamas and one bathing suit. When they needed to wash their clothes they would don their bathing suits, pile their dirty clothes into the dinghy and row to the nearest freshwater pool, stream or small waterfall, where they would proceed to scrub the signs of their travels off their clothing. For eating, they each had one cup and one plate, which they dutifully cleaned in the ocean. The bedding was stored under Elizabeth's bunk and the food under Capi's bed, next to the gas tank. David slept in the half-metre gap between the two. Order and tidiness are important in a boat, and woe betide the person who asks another to get off the storage locker one more time, because they forgot to get something out the last time they were in there.

As there was neither refrigeration nor an icebox for perishables, they took mostly dried food, condensed milk, jam, some canned

Facing page: David and Peter, Welcome Pass, Thormanby Islands, 1929. COURTESY JANET BLANCHET

butter and canned bacon. Thought had to be given to the stowage of their gear and food. It might be tempting to put items that are used most often within easy reach, but heavier objects need to be close to the waterline and distributed equally on both sides of the boat to maintain proper stability. An organized system is essential. Living so close to the water brings additional problems: boats leak, the air is moist and condensation is a constant; it can take a wet sock a week to dry out under such conditions. If the dried stores are not packed in airtight containers they become soggy and damp. A box of opened crackers might last two days before they are limp and squashy, and oatmeal, a staple for boaters, can quickly turn into a soft mass of sticky dough. Even gulls, the scavengers of cruisers' refuse, know better than to eat such proffered morsels of mush.

As for fresh food, Capi and the children met occasional homesteaders from whom they could buy eggs, or whatever fresh fruit or vegetables were growing in their gardens. They gathered berries

along their walks, sometimes hiking all day just to get to a known patch of delicious, bright-red huckleberries. The sea was rich in food: halibut, lingcod, rockfish and flat fish, sweet Dungeness crab, red and green sea urchins, prawns and shrimp, delicious butter clams and robust mussels were freely available. They did take advantage of some of these delicacies, but seafood was not one of Capi's preferred foods. It was not the taste as much the fishy smell that she objected to. Joan once caught a beautiful salmon and gave it to her mother for supper. Capi, being resourceful, baked it outside on a cedar shake, which effectively eliminated the offending odours. The use of the cedar shake had another benefit, as the cooking "pan" could be put directly into the fire after use, thus doing away with the need to wash up. Capi put the other fishy dishes and cutlery in a tidal pool so that little crabs could clean them off.

They had a ready source of drinking water, because they could collect it from the many freshwater lakes and streams along the coast. No one paid much attention to the possibility of ingesting Giardia, Cryptosporidium or Escherichia coli, all naturally occurring common protozoa and bacteria found in wilderness waters; they were a hardy lot. Their food was cooked on a two-burner Coleman stove that sat on the steering seat, and the area for food preparation was about the same size as a child's toy kitchen.

It is unimaginable how difficult this must have been. There was no place to put anything and nothing was handy. If something needed for cooking was not out, it might mean moving charts, bedding or bodies to retrieve it from where it was neatly stored. If it were not worth the effort, two of the five ingredients needed

Facing page, top: Sunbathing while the laundry dries. Bottom: Joan in the dinghy, Wilson Creek, Sechelt Peninsula. COURTESY JANET BLANCHET for a recipe would have to suffice. It was camping, not gourmet feasting. In contrast, many boats that cruise the coast today have such conveniences as refrigerators, freezers, ice-makers, dishwashers, microwave ovens, built-in stoves, plug-in tea kettles and espresso makers; life at sea is a lot less like camping than like living in a luxurious floating hotel.

Once the boat was provisioned it was time to think about navigational instruments and other marine aids necessary for safe transit in ocean waters. Capi had to find space to stow quite a number of marine charts, which are both large and cumbersome. Today, charts are rolled for storage and tucked up in the crossbars in the cabin's headliner, like lined-up pencils; they are out of the way, easily accessible and not likely to get torn or damaged. The *Caprice* had pliable canvas for its deckhead, so Capi probably had to fold her charts and tuck them into a locker or under a bunk when they were not in use. The problem with folding a chart is that creases can mask an important marker that might warn of danger.

Most boats now have chart tables large enough to comfortably plot out a course, but there was no room in the *Caprice* for such a luxury. Fixing a course must have been a cumbersome and unwieldy job for Capi. Juggling dividers and parallel rulers to set out course, time, speed and distance, on an 86-by-119-centimetre chart, possibly damp, in a tiny space would be trying. Capi might have appreciated the neatly folded compact charts that were issued by the Canadian Hydrographic Service in 1962, in response to boaters' requests for something smaller, and she might be surprised to learn that, seventy years after her boating time, paper charts would be dismissed as the product of a bygone era. In their place electronic chart displays with an attendant Global Positioning System plot a boat's location with pinpoint accuracy and track its movement relative to the shoreline. If the system crashes, however, boaters may have to wait in some out-of-the-way place while another is flown in, all of which is time-consuming and costly; paper charts are still a good back-up.

Capi's cruising charts could have been either British Admiralty charts or those produced by the Canadian Hydrographic Service. The British Admiralty published charts for BC waters from the mid-1800s through to the 1950s, although some of the locations that Capi visited had not seen any revisions on the charts since the late 1800s. Most of the charts would have been fairly accurate, with one exception. The infamous Nakwakto Rapids and the waters beyond, in Seymour Inlet, Belize Inlet and Alison Sound, were not surveyed until the 1950s and were not fully detailed until 1982. Charts were not available for the area until 1987, many years after Capi's expedition. In order to successfully negotiate the Nakwakto Rapids she had to rely on a combination of grit and local knowledge. In the main, however, the BC coast has been well served by a number of very good hydrographers, from Juan Perez in 1774 to Captain George Vancouver, who made extensive surveys in 1792 and 1793.

The excellence of those early surveyors and the charts they produced facilitate safe navigation. But a caveat remains, for, despite the best efforts of the Canadian Hydrographic Service, there is bound to be the odd uncharted rock or anomaly. Vigilance is needed when cruising this coast. Capi was well aware of this and took precautions in her navigation, though she sometimes felt frustrated. "You may have taken fixes on distant points or trees, and think you have worked out a passage," she explained. "But the boulders have anticipated this . . . At low tide there is perhaps six feet of water over the sand—sometimes more, sometimes less—but no one ever knows how much over the boulders."[9] Capi had a keen eye and was quick to learn. The entrances to many of the inlets and small coves on the coast lie hidden behind tangles of trees and confusing arrays of islets. This creates a kind of optical illusion that erases form and dimension; from afar the land looks featureless. Furthermore, a veil of sea fog often all but closes the approaches, obscuring the land markings even more. Before Capi went into an anchorage, she studied the landscape thoroughly, taking note of the contour and position of the mountains. From a distance they can look like a series of creases, only height and shadow distinguishing one peak from another. Capi said, "Navigators approaching strange shores, and confronted with a solid line of mountains, know . . . that if they approach a mountain of a certain altitude, with other mountains that fold in a certain way on to either side—then a certain sound or harbour will open out as they approach closer."[10]

Capi's navigational instruments were crude but effective—rocks, fishing line, whistles and local help saw her through most incidents. When entering a bay or preparing to anchor, she used the age-old method of sounding the bottom. She fashioned a lead line out of fishing line and a rock, which she would throw over the side to check the depth of the water. A lead line is a simple instrument in which a length of cotton or manila line is wound around a spool and has a "lead" or weight spliced to one end. Strips of leather, twine and coloured cloth are tied to the line at various intervals, each representing a particular depth. As a ship entered a port or neared a shoreline the lead line was dropped over the side; when the weight hit the bottom the leadsman read the line and called out the depth. Both Captain Cook and Captain Vancouver used lead lines when charting the BC coast. As easy as the procedure seems, lead lines provide only a partial description of the seabed: crucial shoals and other significant underwater hazards can easily be missed.

As an added safeguard, Capi would row around an anchorage in her dinghy, looking for submerged reefs or kelp that often marks treacherous rocks. Only when she was satisfied that the *Caprice* was in a safe location would she set the anchor. Sometimes, however, even these precautions failed. She wrote of the time when they were anchored off 'Mi'mkwamlis (Village Island), waiting for their chance to go up Knight Inlet. The chart had indicated that there was good holding ground, so they anchored in what they thought was five metres of water. While she did investigate the anchorage, Capi was not as careful as she normally was—it was late and the water was murky. "We woke to an embarrassing situation," she wrote. "We found ourselves

Facing page: Rocks exposed at low tide, a typical hazard on the coast.

trapped in a little pool . . . and surrounded by reefs that we could hardly see over."[11] A homesteader from the area, an old Norwegian, appeared in the bay and told them that they had anchored in too far and they could expect to be trapped for another two or three hours until the tide rose. They felt foolish but were thankful they had not gone aground. Even with today's depth sounders, which provide the boater with a detailed contour of the ocean bottom, groundings are still a concern. According to the Transportation Safety Board, in the first ten months of 2006 there were already ninety-four reported such incidents in Canadian waters. Even large vessels, handled by professional mariners, can end up running aground: in March 2006, the *Queen of the North*, a BC ferry, ran aground on Gill Island in Wright Sound and sank in 430 metres of water.

Dense fog is a common occurrence in the summer months and will sweep the inlets and bays with its hazy tentacles in the blink of an eye. It dampens sound, hides boats from each other and can be alarmingly disorienting, presenting an extreme danger to marine traffic. Radar and marine radios are essential for operating in such conditions. Capi had neither. She employed an old technique that mariners have used for centuries: whistling or shouting and then listening, counting the number of seconds an echo takes. Sound has to travel from the vessel to the object and back again, and as its speed through the air is 335 metres per second, an echo returning after five seconds would indicate a distance off of approximately half a mile. While this works in principle, it is not something that boaters want to have to rely on; under the circumstances Capi had no choice. Once, David used this technique to good effect when the *Caprice* was nearing Deep Sea Bluff, at the eastern entrance to

Facing page: A fog bank, another hazard to coastal travel.

Simoom Sound. They found themselves suddenly enshrouded by fog and lost all contact with the lay of the land. Capi wrote, "He [David] gathered up all the breath he had in his body—and a mighty blast fared forth into the void. We were all poised to count the seconds—but we had hardly started before back it bounced . . . I hastily kicked the engine into neutral." Directly in front of them was a towering, thirty-metre, vertically striated cliff. "'Why, it's Deep Sea Bluff,' I practically shouted. I hadn't realized we were so far north."[12]

Whenever she could, Capi talked to fishermen, loggers, trappers and homesteaders about the best channels, approaches or anchorages to use, adding their experience to her reservoir of information. She learned from old Mike, a homesteader in Melanie Cove, not to anchor beyond the copper mark on the cliff as the water shallows quickly.

On a run up to Seymour Inlet, she had to turn from the sheltering waters of Wells Passage into the open waters of Queen Charlotte Strait with its accompanying swell. The *Caprice* was not built for a beam sea, and this passage would be uncomfortable; it would take about two hours before she could tuck in behind the Raynor Group, which would give them shelter until they reached the entrance to Blunden Harbour. Capi needed an alternative route. Loggers had told her of a deep-water passage between the shore and a reef that would take them up as far as Blunden Harbour, an old route used by the Kwakwaka'wakw people in small boats or canoes. The *Caprice* had a shallow draft and should have been able to transit the pass, but this required studied concentration and running with one foot on the beach. "I made out a line of kelp extending along the coast," Capi wrote. "I worked in closer . . . we came to a gap with no kelp and evidently no reef . . . We slipped

Facing page: Steep cliff, similar to Deep Sea Bluff.

through on top of a swell . . . and here certainly was the Indian channel . . . It seemed deep right up to the shore."[13] The chart does not show any such reef system and Capi admitted as much. The water is deep quite close to the shore but the tidal variations average four metres and there are many off-lying rocks. They made it to Blunden Harbour, partly with luck, particularly given the strong currents and fog common to the area.

Blunden Harbour would have provided the best protection for them, but they were anxious to get as far as the Southgate Islands, a further twenty-four kilometres up the coast. They gave Blunden Harbour a glancing look and somewhat reluctantly continued on. They were pressing their luck: usually by mid-morning the prevailing northwesterlies freshen and the seas build; they can be particularly nasty on an opposing tide. But good fortune was still on their side;

the winds remained light and they headed out again into the open swells of Queen Charlotte Strait. In all it probably took them more than five hours to get to their destination. It was an exhausting trip, frightening at times. They were also hungry. The ups and downs of the ocean waves made it difficult to cobble together a lunch of any sort. Reflecting on their experience, Capi wrote, "The rollers were distinctly alarming at times. Very frightening when they suddenly broke right ahead of you on a completely hidden rock . . . The reef would show for a moment in the hollow, and it wasn't hard to see what would have happened to our boat if we had been there."[14]

Sometimes it was a combination of nail-biting and tempered control that got them through a particularly nasty patch of water: going through the Nakwakto Rapids to see what lay beyond is a case in point. The rapids are northeast of Port Hardy on the mainland side, where there are few secure anchorages.

On the evening before their run up through the rapids, Capi talked to a fisheries inspector she had met about the best way to negotiate the strong tidal stream. Nakwakto has an impressive sea surface slope and dangerous reefs that extend out from Turret Rock. Turret Rock, known locally as Tremble Island, lies in the middle of the rapids and splits the channel in two. When the current is in its full fury it can reach 14.5 knots on a maximum ebb tide, causing the island to tremble. It was critical for Capi to have the *Caprice* positioned appropriately, ready to go through on the first of the slack water as there is only six minutes before the tide turns. The sailing directions provide a cautionary note: "Mariners are strongly advised to navigate Nakwakto Rapids only at slack water for at no other time

Facing page: Copper stain on rock in Melanie Cove. Capi was told not to anchor beyond this.

is it possible to navigate these rapids safely."[15] The *Canadian Tide and Current Tables* contain a warning that the predictions may be affected by geographic or meteorological conditions. An important factor not calculated into them is that the time of the turn to ebb can be significantly influenced by the amount of rain occurring in the mountains above the shoreline. As the rain cascades down the valleys and drains into the inlets, it can cause the time of the turn to ebb to be earlier, by as much as an hour. Several boats have not taken this into account and swirled around helplessly until the rapids released their grasp. Capi needed to work out her time, distance and speed over the ground precisely, and even then it would be a risky venture for a boat as lightly built as the *Caprice*.

The fisheries inspector had told Capi that the best advice he could give her would be to turn around and go back. As an extra deterrent he relayed his own experience with the rapids on the previous evening. He had missed slack water by about twenty minutes but thought he could still get through. As soon as he entered the current he realized he had made a mistake. His boat was caught up in the swirls and bashed against a cliff so hard that the impact sheared off the propeller. What little control he had was lost, and he was at the mercy of reversing waterfalls and boiling cauldrons of water. For the next five or six hours he was churned and twisted and knocked about until both his bow and stern splintered. He then spent the night bailing furiously, trying to keep his boat afloat, until the early hours of the morning at the next slack water. It was an interesting story, Capi thought. She was not at all dissuaded, though it did cause her some concern.

She wrote, "I am supposed to look calm and collected at such moments . . . I was busy furtively arguing with myself . . . We were used to all the other narrows on the coast . . . and how flat they were at slack! . . . If we hadn't met the inspector I wouldn't be thinking any of this."[16] She stepped up her preparations. She checked and rechecked everything, cleaned both the spark plugs and the points on the magneto and fed the children their lunch. They slipped through without a worry. "We went gently through . . . The channel opened out into a comparatively wide section," she wrote. "Then the swirls began to form around us—the six minutes must be up. But we were through . . . Peter shook his head sagely, 'You were scared, too, weren't you Mummy?' I winked at him. 'Weren't we sillies!' I said."[17]

CHAPTER THREE ✤

Cruising Princess Louisa Inlet and Desolation Sound

More than seventy summers have passed since Capi and her children cruised the inlets and waterways along the Strait of Georgia, Johnstone Strait and Queen Charlotte Strait. Much has changed and yet much has stayed the same since they carved their dreams into the fabric of time. The people she wrote about have slipped from Earth; some have left traces, others not. Places she knew appear familiar and yet different—sometimes there is a vague outline of what was, of what they saw.

At the top end of Princess Louisa Inlet and west of Chatterbox Falls there is a spot called Trappers Rock where Capi and the children often tied up. The first year they found their way into this pristine, glacier-cut terrain they had the anchorage nearly to themselves, just the way they liked it. It was an exciting find for the family. In their previous reading about the area, the children were delighted to learn that Captain George Vancouver had missed the entrance, assuming it was a creek instead. They saw themselves as intrepid explorers, discovering places unknown. Princess Louisa Inlet is almost indescribable in its beauty. It is approached by way of Jervis Inlet, a deep fjord that slices into the Coast Range and divides the Sunshine Coast in two.

Facing page: Aerial view of Princess Louisa Inlet. COURTESY BC ARCHIVES

91

It is an area where katabatic winds typically sweep down from the mountaintops, spilling out into the inlet and over the boats below. Capi battled the wind part of the way up, but the *Caprice* held firm, inching its way along. Relaying her experience, she wrote, "[The wind] picks you up in its teeth and shakes you. It hits you first on one side and then on the other. There is nowhere to go, you just have to take it."[1]

Princess Louisa Inlet is entered at its south end, through Malibu Rapids, a narrow gorge where the waters are squeezed, causing overfalls and whirlpools. The tidal stream in Malibu Rapids can attain 9 knots during large tides, and it is best traversed in mid-channel, at slack or near slack water. Capi negotiated this passage aggressively but without much finesse. She wrote that it was "an effort to control the boat . . . as you race past the last points, the ridge shatters into a turmoil of a dozen different currents and confusions. Your boat dashes toward the rocky cliff . . . the cliff . . . rushes toward your boat. You wrestle with the wheel . . . and finally manage to drag the two apart."[2] The inlet then provides a four-mile cruise alongside upthrustings of Precambrian granite and tree-covered mountains that rise to heights of 2,100 metres. At its head is one of the most famous waterfalls in British Columbia: Chatterbox Falls, a forty-metre raging force of water that snakes down from the headwaters of Loquilts Creek and plunges with great clamour into the still waters below.[3]

On the Blanchets' first visit there was only one inhabitant in the inlet, a German army deserter named Herman Casper. It was said that you could pick up a flea or two from him. He was a blacksmith, zither player and master of twenty-six cats, but he lived down at the mouth of the inlet, by Malibu Rapids; he was no bother. In the main, they were free to explore without interference, so they were slightly miffed the following year when they found the "intruder," as they called him, building a cabin in their spot. Capi noted this infringement with smouldering contempt. "On the other side of the falls we could see a big float . . . new since last year. Somewhere in behind lay the log cabin and the intruder . . . this man and his log-cabin made the first thin wedge of civilization that had been driven into our favourite inlet."[4, 5] The intruder was James Frederick "Mac" Macdonald who had struck it rich in the Nevada mining boom.[6] He had first visited Princess Louisa Inlet in 1919 and fallen in love with the area. After his windfall he was able to purchase the property at the head of the inlet. In 1927 he paid $420 to the BC government for a small piece of rock and a forest of trees a hundred miles from civillization.

Despite the incursion into her quiet anchorage, Capi had to admit that she was impressed by the quality of work and thought that had gone into the construction of Mac's house. Very spacious inside, unlike many on the coast, it was elegant yet rustic. It was built entirely of peeled cedar logs, as was much of the furniture. He had a large stone fireplace, beautiful shiny wood floors and a handsome stairway that led up to the bedrooms and bathroom. There were floor-to-ceiling bookshelves and a lovely Navajo-looking throw rug on the floor, creating a very comfortable and inviting home, much like the man himself. Always a gracious host, he entertained boaters, loggers, trappers and fishermen, telling them stories of the history and legends of the inlet and pointing out places of interest and of danger. Capi and the children returned several times during their summer cruises. Her initial ambivalence toward and disdain of the man gradually turned into friendship, and she and Mac had many interesting chats over the years. However, as boaters began visiting the area more frequently, Capi and the children spent less time there. Where once they had stayed several weeks, they later confined their visit to a number of days. Beautiful though it was, the inlet was becoming too populated for her.

Over time Mac's name became synonymous with the inlet. He grew to become its protector, acting as a self-appointed custodian; he built hiking trails, floats, ramps and outdoor fireplaces to add to the comfort of his visitors. Above all else, Mac wanted "the Princess" to remain unspoiled, and he worked hard to preserve the area in its natural state. Despite many offers to purchase his land he stayed, even when his cabin was destroyed by fire in 1940. At one point, in the early 1950s, he was offered $400,000. He could have used the money, as he was then running short, but the land was not for sale. Mac was concerned about the very real possibility that his beloved inlet could be used for commercial interests. It had happened once before, in the late 1930s.

A wealthy investor, Thomas Hamilton, bought Casper's place for $500.[7] It was not long before saws and axes could be heard throughout the inlet; trees were felled and land was cleared. Barges clogged the area, bringing in building supplies and the sand—tons of it—needed to lay the surface for an eighteen-hole golf course. Hamilton was building a luxury resort. When it was finished he named it the Malibu Club, after his yacht, *Malibu*. The resort was to be part of an exclusive yacht-charter service for Hollywood stars and millionaires. John F. Kennedy, Bob Hope, Bing Crosby and John Wayne were among the visitors to the Malibu Club. After World War II, when there was a downturn in tourism, the club could no longer sustain itself and Hamilton had to abandon the project. He originally offered the resort for sale for $1,000,000 but sold it in 1953 for $300,000 to an enterprise called Young Life, which turned it into a non-denominational camp for teens. Young Life still operates the Malibu Club and continues to provide young people with an exceptional wilderness experience.

Mac tended "the Princess" until he could no longer afford to do so. Feeling strongly that Princess Louisa Inlet should belong to no one individual, he deeded his property in 1953 to the boaters of the Pacific Northwest under the guardianship of the non-profit Princess Louisa International Society. In 1965 the British Columbia Parks Department took over the administration of the area and made it into a marine park. The Princess Louisa International Society continues to function as an advisory body and has added more land to the park. In 2003, with the Nature Conservancy of Canada and a number of other organizations, it purchased an additional eighty-nine hectares surrounding Mac's original land.

The park continues to be accessible to the boating public. There is a public float with sixty metres of dock space, a rainy-day shelter named the James F. Macdonald Memorial Lodge and more than eight hundred metres of trails and boardwalks at Chatterbox Falls. The climb up to the top of Chatterbox Falls is invigorating, and it can be quite slippery. In that respect, it has not changed much since Capi and the children hiked to the falls. Her description is still accurate. "We climbed up beside the falls," she wrote. "The stream above was very turbulent—you would certainly be battered to death on the big boulders if you fell in. And if you escaped that, there were the falls below to finish you off."[8] Twelve people have fallen to their deaths from the top of the falls and the parks department has now put up a sign that reads, "Do not go near the top of the falls. The surrounding flat rocks are moss covered and slippery. 12 people have lost their lives by not observing this warning."

Outside the park there still is a trail that leads to Trappers Cabin, to which Capi and the children hiked. Their destination was beyond the cabin and the traplines, up 1,200 metres of seemingly impenetrable mountain boulders, slippery moss and thorny devil's club, and around bears' dens. They were looking for a particularly luscious patch of huckleberry bushes that Capi said had berries twice the size of black

currants. It takes about two hours, scrambling up six hundred metres of demanding terrain, to reach Trappers Cabin. *Waggoner Cruising Guide* gets it right when it warns, "Climbing the trail to the trapper's cabin is like taking the stairs to the top of the Sears Tower—twice—with a boot-camp training obstacle on every third landing."[9] And it is easy to get lost as there are many side trails. However, the view down the inlet is breathtaking—it is well worth the climb. The parks department warns that it is for experienced hikers only, and it certainly tested the determination of Capi and the children. "The road slanted at quite an incline," she wrote, "and every muscle screamed with the punishment before we got there . . . We had to stop to get our breath every hundred feet or so." Once they were at the cabin they dropped, exhausted. The hike up to Trappers Cabin is enough of a challenge in itself; to go farther is to hike on wobbly legs and spent energy. After they caught their breath they pressed on, beyond the trail—resting, slipping, resting some more until they came to the edge of a flat near the end of the treeline, where they found their sought-after huckleberries; sun-drenched, delicious and sweet. "You just milked them off the bushes. And then we just sat and ate and ate and ate."[10]

Most of the Blanchets' summers were spent exploring Desolation Sound. It is a boaters' paradise and was a perfect place for the family. The weather was pleasant, the swimming enjoyable and the sheltered waters allowed Pam, the Gordon Setter, to move out of the main boat and take up residence in the dinghy. The *Caprice* was really too small for its cargo, so when they could, they towed Pam behind. It must have been a spectacle of some amusement to see a small boat, filled to the gunwales with people, towing a dog from anchorage to anchorage.

Desolation Sound is nestled against the western edge of the Coast Range and is accessible only by water or air. It is about three hundred kilometres up the coast from Capi's home. If she were to have gone directly to Desolation Sound from Curteis Point, it would have taken her about thirty-four hours, travelling non-stop.[11] She didn't, of course; they were in no hurry.

Capi kept a copy of Captain George Vancouver's journal onboard as a reference source, "filling in the few gaps in our knowledge," she wrote.[12] Part of their winter activities was to read about the places they would visit during the summer; it added more interest to their trips and acted as a learning tool for the children's schoolwork. They studied the ethnology and archaeology of early anthropologists, but Captain Vancouver's account was still one of the best sources of information on cruising the coast. Unlike today, when there are more books offering advice and direction than any one person has time to read, cruising guides were not readily available in Capi's time.

The rather ominous name of Desolation Sound belies the exquisite beauty of the area. It is a place of spectacular waterfalls, countless islands, beautiful bays and coves, saltwater lagoons and deep-cut mountains with sheer facades. Rounding the corner from the Malaspina Peninsula and entering the great glacial basin, a boater is welcomed by a line of snow-topped mountains that overlook the sound, like primordial titans of the heavens. It received its gloomy name from Captain Vancouver. Although he was there at the end of June in 1792, he found the surroundings bleak, isolated and inhospitable. The weather was uncooperative, the winds were unpredictable and their ships' anchors dragged. It was hard to take soundings because the coastline was rugged and mountains precipitous. They were attacked by fleas and were running low on food: they could not find even so much as a berry to eat or a fish to catch. "Our residence here was truly forlorn," he wrote, "an awful silence pervaded the gloomy forests, whilst animated nature seemed to have deserted the neighbouring country."[13]

Since Capi and the children last visited Desolation Sound, it has become a major destination for boaters from all over the world. People come for the beauty and for the many sheltered anchorages that dot the inlets. The waters are reported to be the warmest on the coast, reaching up to 26°C in the summer months, ideal for swimming. When Capi rounded Sarah Point for the first time, there was little traffic. She could tuck up into Squirrel Cove, Teakerne Arm or Theodosia Inlet and have the anchorage to herself. The family did meet up with people, and from time to time joined other boaters on short jaunts to one place or another. Now, however, anchorages are filled with boats of every description. For the 2006 summer season, the parks department reported that more than

Facing page, top: Entrance to Melanie Cove. Bottom: The *Caprice* and the *Ivanhoe*. COURTESY JANET BLANCHET

10,500 boats visited Desolation Sound.[14] In Melanie Cove, a jewel of an anchorage and one that Capi particularly enjoyed, there can be as many as fifty boats at any one time. When Capi anchored in the cove there was only Mike, whom she liked, a cougar that terrified Pam, and Phil Lavine, an old Frenchman who lived in Laura Cove, less than a kilometre down the path from Mike.[15]

Capi always looked forward to seeing Mike, an old logger from Michigan. His name was really Andrew Shuttler, but no one called him that. When Capi first met him she thought he looked like Honoré Daumier's portrayal of Don Quixote, with his aquiline nose, pointed forehead and handlebar moustache. But rather than sporting an ancient shield and riding a skinny old horse with a fast greyhound at his side, Mike wore logging clothes and had a lumberjack style about him; his steed was a rowboat and he had no animals, as cougars prowled the area. Like Don Quixote he loved books. Capi always made sure that she tucked in some interesting reading material for him when she left home. He particularly liked the classics and enjoyed reading early philosophers. Capi brought him books and magazines that would be difficult for him to obtain in the wilderness, and their contents sparked many lively discussions between them.

Mike's place at the head of the inlet was a small oasis of flowers and fruit. Up the bank, he had built himself a pleasant homestead, and he worked hard clearing the land and keeping the constantly encroaching forest at bay. The hillside was planted with apple trees, grapes, honeysuckle, sweet william and bleeding-hearts, which, when they were in bloom, sent a heady fragrance wafting over the water. His log cabin was surrounded by terraced rows of flowers. Mike could always tell when the *Caprice* was due for

Facing page: View of Mike's place.

its annual visit: when the orchard was bursting with apples Capi and the children would come puttering into the bay and set their anchor. Mike would stand at the head of the cove, his well-worn black felt hat shadowing his face, with his usual greeting of, "Well, well, well! Summer's here, and here you are again!" Everyone looked forward to their visit with Mike, and the children knew that there would be a delicious apple pie or two to indulge in.

Then one summer, as they rounded the corner and squeezed past the drying ledge that projects from the south shore of Melanie Point, something was not quite right; the anchorage felt empty, devoid of life. Mike was not there to greet them and when they went up to his cabin they found it empty. Worse yet, it had been stripped of all but a rusty stove and a few letters and cards that were scattered about. Mike had taken ill and spent his last days in the hospital in Powell River.

Born in 1858 in Minnesota, he was seventy-three when he died in 1931. A great sadness overtook the family as they realized that they would see him no more. "The cove rang like an empty seashell," Capi wrote. "A great northern raven, which can carry on a conversation with all the intonations of the human voice, blew out from above the cabin, excitedly croaking, 'Mike's dead! Mike's dead'."[16]

Mike's place is all but gone now, and red alders, ferns and bracken have moved in, covering up the tracks of a man who for thirty-eight years called Melanie Cove his home. In a small section at the end of the cove, the terraced areas that Mike built up, stone by stone, can still be found, and off to the right of the path, near the parks department's biffy, there are a few apple trees left, although they, too, are surrendering to the creeping clamber of lichens.

One other person whom Capi used to visit was Phil Lavine, who was in his seventies when she first met him. He had a homestead in Laura Cove, around the corner from Mike. He and Mike were friends so, rather than hopping into a boat every time they wanted to see each other, they built a trail to connect the two homesteads. Phil had a shady past; he was said to have killed a man in Quebec. But on the coast, far from the site of his wrongdoings, he lived modestly on a small old-age pension of twenty dollars a month. He raised chickens and goats, tended his vegetable garden and grew his own tobacco.

Capi used to buy fresh eggs from Phil and always got a yarn into the bargain. Phil could not read a word, but the winter Mike died—when the nights were short and storms raged—he carefully shepherded all of his friend's books to his own place, as a sort of memorial to Mike. He built bookshelves around the cabin and proudly displayed

Facing page, top: View from Mike's place. Bottom: All that is left of Mike's place, today.

the books for all to see. "All dem words, and 'e ad to die like all de rest of us!" he told Capi.[17] At Phil's place today, there is little left of his homestead except for a bit of the cabin, which is increasingly hidden by the forest. The path between Mike's and Phil's is still there, although it is a little convoluted and not particularly easy to follow.

There have been other changes in Desolation Sound, as well. There are now scores of tour companies that take people to see the sights and to experience the wilderness; there are natural-history tours, kayaking expeditions, summer camps, Elderhostels, resorts and marinas. Pit toilets have been constructed in Prideaux Haven, Tenedos Bay and Grace Harbour, and there is a garbage scow in Refuge Cove. At Refuge Cove boaters can fuel up or shop for groceries at the quaint general store. People can also have a hot shower, do laundry, buy a mouth-watering cinnamon roll or blueberry scone, drink a latté or swap stories on the dock with other travellers. As its name implies, it is a refuge where everyone eventually meets up. Capi did stop in at Refuge Cove but she might not have been too keen on jostling among contentious boaters, as happens today, waiting for a place alongside.

The area has masses of shellfish, which mattered little to Capi as she would have none of it. The water quality and warmth are ideal for oyster-growing operations, scallop leases and geoduck farming. Along with those enterprises comes serious debate among various interest groups about the ecological implications of aquaculture. There are six marine parks: Copeland Islands, Desolation Sound on the Gilford Peninsula, Roscoe Bay, Walsh

Facing page: Refuge Cove Store. Cove and Teakerne Arm on West Redonda Island and Háthaym (Von Donop) on Cortes Island. Desolation Sound Marine Park is the largest; it encompasses 8,449 hectares with sixty kilometres of shoreline and has some

of the most stunning anchorages, including Prideaux Haven, Melanie Cove and Laura Cove. There are also two provincial parks: Malaspina Provincial Park and Tux'wnech Okeover Arm Provincial Park, both on the Malaspina Peninsula.

If it all gets a bit hectic, it is easy to step onto that arc of time once again and drop right back into Capi's time, imagining her and the children stopping for the night at Mink Island and making a fire on the sloping rock to cook their meal, hoping that no unfriendly boats came by because they were eating out-of-season venison. Then, too, this magnificent land of glacial fjords has remained almost unchanged for ten thousand years.

CHAPTER FOUR

Cruising Beyond Desolation Sound

While Capi and the children spent most of their time in and around Desolation Sound, they did venture farther up the coast, anxious to see the lands and villages of the Kwakwaka'wakw before they disappeared. Capi's photographs of this area date from 1936, so the probability is that they visited the northern islands only once. Their interest in the cultures of the First Nations was piqued one winter when they found a stone pestle, a hammer-like tool, buried on their property. While Capi was well versed and read a great deal about the archaeology of coastal British Columbia, she knew nothing about the pestle, other than that it was very old and was most likely an artifact belonging to the Wsanec, the original inhabitants of the Saanich Peninsula. That sent them to the library where they gathered a winter's worth of reading about First Nations anthropology and archaeology.

It would be a challenge for them to travel up into the mythic lands of the raven and the eagle, and a solid knowledge of navigation and meteorology was essential. They would have to face whirlpools, reversing falls, strong currents, turbulent water, shoal patches and rocks. Fog can blanket the inlets for days and days. Capi needed to pay careful attention to the *Canadian Tide and Current Tables* and take the weather into account, as well. The local currents

Facing page: Johnstone Strait.

are strong and are influenced by tides, freshwater run-off and winds.

It is important to know how to perform time, speed and distance calculations and have a good understanding of how to use the tide and current tables. At one point Capi had a series of three rapids to go through—the Yuculta, Dent and Green Point rapids—so she had to be meticulous in her computations. She first had to calculate her speed over the ground, which, due to the current, is different from the speed through the water. She then had to factor in the distance from one set of rapids to the other and take note of the direction of the tidal stream. The *Caprice* was too slow to buck the tide so if Capi wanted to travel in a westerly direction she needed to go with the ebb. Her next step would be to check the times of slack water at the three sets of rapids. She had to base her calculations on two different reference stations, Gillard Passage and Seymour Narrows, and to apply time differences to the reference stations. The Yuculta Rapids turn to flood twenty-five minutes later than the turn at Gillard Passage and to ebb five minutes later; Dent Rapids turn to flood fifteen minutes before the turn at Gillard Passage and to ebb twenty-five minutes before; Green Point Rapids turn to flood one hour and twenty-five minutes earlier than the turn at Seymour Narrows and to ebb one hour and thirty-five minutes earlier. These are not waters to be entered without due care and attention.

There are two ways to approach the north coast by boat, and each requires a passage through Johnstone Strait—a fifty-four-mile stretch of water that that separates Vancouver Island from the mainland. It is a marine highway, part of the Inside Passage, and is flanked by a phalanx of beautiful islands that are clad in cathedral-like forests. The strait can at times be gentle and mystical and at other times fierce and challenging, as gale-force winds funnel down it. Short steep waves, which bunch up like the bellows of a concertina, can batter hulls with an intensity that is unrelenting. Capi didn't like Johnstone Strait. Once, she wrote, "Johnstone Straits were running white—and it wasn't any fun. So we turned off into a narrow harbour to wait it out. We waited for a couple of days. Tied up to a long float that keeled over when the wind hit."[1]

The most direct route to the north is to enter Johnstone Strait through Discovery Passage and go up through Seymour Narrows. The tidal streams in Seymour Narrows attain 16 knots and are characterized by strong eddies, gaping whirlpools and violent rips. When the tide is opposed by a strong wind, the passage becomes extremely dangerous, especially to small vessels, although even big cruise ships need to approach at slack water. Captain Vancouver said that Seymour Narrows was one of the vilest stretches of water in the world. The *Sailing Directions* devote three-quarters of a page to discussing how best to transit the narrows, noting that even during times of slack water, caution must be used. If this is not enough of a warning, there is a provincial sign posted on the highway overlooking Seymour Narrows that reads, in part, "Treacherous currents, swirling eddies, and turbulent tide-rips still harass vessels, despite the blasting away in 1958 of Ripple Rock . . . the Narrows has claimed numerous ships and lives and is considered by many seamen the worst hazard to marine navigation on the British Columbia coast."[2]

In Capi's time there was the added danger of a submerged mountain, with two crests, that jutted up from the ocean floor; it would take the *Caprice* twelve minutes to pass over it. At low water these jagged peaks sat a mere three metres below the surface. This undersea mountain was called Ripple Rock, so named by Captain Richards in 1860 to describe the ebb over the rock. The danger with Ripple Rock was that it was located right in the middle of the

channel, a constricted conduit only a half-mile in width. The current was so strong in Seymour Narrows that it could suck a vessel into the whirlpools and onto the rocks. Ripple Rock and Seymour Narrows claimed 114 lives and 120 vessels over the years. In 1958 the twin tops were blown up in the largest, commercial, non-nuclear explosion of the time. It took 2.5 years of tunnelling through the mountain and up into the peaks to set the load; 1,375 tons of Nitramex 2H were used. The resulting explosion spewed 700,000 tons of rock and water into the air, 305 metres high.

As Capi never wrote about going up Johnstone Strait through Seymour Narrows, it has to be assumed that she chose the less perilous transit through the Yucultas (pronounced "Yew-kuh-taws"). This more northerly route eliminates about thirty kilometres of the worst of Johnstone Strait, but she still had to go through three or four sets of rapids. The Yucultas is a local word that encompasses the

Yuculta Rapids, Gillard Passage, Barber Passage and Dent Rapids, which is the most menacing. At Dent Rapids the channel narrows to 3/10 of a mile and the flood can reach 11 knots. On the flood, a standing wave is formed when the south-going flood stream meets a northerly branch of the flood that has flowed through Tugboat Passage. A whirlpool about nine metres in diameter is created near the standing wave. Capi did write about going through the Yuculta Rapids, but she seemed unconcerned. She said, "You get quite a swirl and strong current when the rapids are running at their hardest, but it is perfectly safe."[3]

On her way through to Johnstone Strait, Capi stopped in at Stuart Island to visit with some people she had met there in previous years. Stuart Island, just north of Desolation Sound at the entrance to Bute Inlet, cannot be approached without passing through at least one set of rapids. The Yuculta Rapids flank its western shores and Arran Rapids its northern end. Despite the fact that Stuart Island is eighty kilometres from Vancouver and was accessible only by boat, it was a busy community in the 1920s and 30s. The Blanchets stopped by several times over the years, and the last time they did, around a hundred people were living there. One of the things that Capi and the children liked to do was to hike up to Eagle Lake, a small lake about forty-five minutes from the head of Big Bay. At the end of the hike was the promise of a swim in warm water, though the path to the lake was marshy and spongy. They found that if they stood for too long in one spot they would start sinking into the boggy water, so they changed into their bathing suits while they were on the move. Eagle Lake was not the nicest lake for a summer dip. Not all of the lakes on the islands are picture-postcard, pristine

Facing page: Seymour Narrows at slack tide.

bodies of aquamarine-coloured water. Many are choked with logs; submerged stumps, slimy and creepy, poke from below and muddy bottoms suck at feet. But Capi and the

Facing page: Sonora Island Resort.

children were always game for a good swim. "It was a peculiar little lake in the middle of . . . muskeg," Capi wrote. "We would . . . ooze into the water, which was warm and very soft. I don't think the lake was very deep, we never investigated closely. We didn't like that bottom—it was soft and sinking, and full of unknowns."[4]

Stuart Island has been a fishing hub for over a century. As far back as 1907 boats vied with one another for position, fishing the rips with the hopes of catching the "big one." One evening Capi left the children playing while she went out to fish with her friends at the edge of the whirlpools. They fished from an old scow that was anchored at one end while the other end was tied to a tree. "The current was so strong that it carried the line out and down . . . the scow twisted this way and that way, and when they saw an extra large whirlpool approaching, the men would slack off on the anchor end and rapidly pull us out of reach with the shore line."[5] They could see all the way down the whirlpool's throat, she said. The fishing was good that day. A man across from them caught a 27-kilogram salmon and they landed an 18-kilogram one—enough to feed a third of the island if they wanted to. Fishing was the reason people came to the area. The recreational-fishing industry experienced a huge growth in the 1930s and has continued ever since.

Stuart Island now has exclusive fishing lodges and large private estates, one of which has a nine-hole golf course. There is a paved private airstrip and a marina, and a night's stay at a lodge can cost as much as eight hundred dollars. Just opposite Stuart Island, on Sonora Island,

an elegant modern resort and spa has been built on a point of land overlooking the Yuculta Rapids. It is West Coast Ritz in the middle of the wilderness. They offer helicopter tours to the tops of glaciers or set a fisherman down in a river for an early morning of fly-fishing. There are tennis courts, a golf course and even a Japanese garden. At the end of the day a massage or a soak in the hot tub is available. It is not hard to imagine what Capi's thoughts might be on such developments.

After visiting the friends at Stuart Island, Capi set off northward and eventually found her way into Johnstone Strait, a stretch of strong winds and choppy seas; the waves here can build anywhere from one to four metres, depending on the direction of the tidal stream and wind. The *Caprice* was taking a good beating and Capi needed to run for cover. She managed to find an anchorage, and although she was a bit vague in the book about where they took shelter, she provided enough clues to suggest that it was Port Neville. The western portion of Johnstone Strait has very few protected anchorages and those are

only temporary at best; there weren't a lot of options. Over the years, Port Neville has sheltered thousands of boats escaping from nasty conditions in the strait and it was perfect for a small boat like the *Caprice*.

Port Neville looks tranquil and is well away from the mainstream. It is the kind of place that makes visitors feel that they have discovered something quite unique, that they are among the very few to have visited. There is no question that it is hard to get to. It is a long way up the coast from Vancouver or Victoria, and boats usually turn into Port Neville after a good thrashing in the straits. Yet people from all over the world have cruised into the inlet and tied up to the red dock to buy supplies, post a letter, seek refuge or to visit with the Hansens. Old Mrs. Hansen, one of the early residents, told of a time in the 1950s when a yacht came into the inlet and tied up at the wharf. The skipper looked around and thought that he was in a remote backwater. He said quite assuredly, "Well this is a place where I don't know anybody," and then introduced himself, saying he was from Belcarra, a small community at the eastern end of Burrard Inlet in Vancouver. Mr. Hansen, who by this time was blind, answered with a quick retort. "Bellcarra, [sic] where the sun shines on both sides of the fence . . . I used to live there." He then went on to say, "I rented the farm from your dad, Judge Bole, for a time and often bounced you on my knee."[6] It is a common misperception that the coast is an isolated area whose inhabitants are ignorant of current affairs and paparazzi-pursued personalities, but to meet the Who's Who of the world, spend some time there.

Facing page: Store and post office at Port Neville.

A landlocked inlet twenty-five kilometres long, Port Neville is tucked securely into the mainland coast. It is filled with kelp forests and clam beaches and is a natural feeding area for crabs, seals and dolphins. Eagles use it as nesting habitat for their young. At the head of the inlet, a wetland estuary is fed by the Fulmore River; it offers an over-wintering site for both marine and shore birds and is one of the few in the area that supports sockeye salmon stocks. About half a mile from the entrance, on the eastern side, there is a public float. It is not the best of places in westerly winds but does offer protection from easterlies. A strong tidal stream runs along the wharf, making landing difficult at times. Port Neville is a contrast of colours and sounds and has an interesting history.

Facing page: The Columbia Coast Mission hospital ship, the Columbia III. *This is not the ship to which Capi sent the message—it was built in 1953—but it served the same purposes along the coast.*

At the head of the dock an old, two-storey log building looks as if it has a tale to tell, which indeed it does. It was built in 1924 by Hans and Kathinka Hansen and is significant because it was the first store north of Vancouver. It was once a thriving store and post office, serving a community of settlers, loggers and boaters. Although the post office is still in operation, the store has been scaled down to a small gift shop. The Hansens supplied the outlying communities with most of the provisions needed for survival in the wilderness. Astute business people, they also had a fuel dock and a contract with Standard Oil to act as agents for the area. The old Union steamships made Port Neville a port-of-call to pick up and deliver mail, people and goods. The post office has the distinction of being the oldest one operating in British Columbia: it was opened in 1895 and is currently run by the granddaughter of Hans Hansen, the original postmaster and one of the pioneers of the inlet.

When Capi and the children had bedded down for the night, secure in their choice of an anchorage, it turned out to be a short night for them. About 3:00 in the morning they were awakened by one of the young Hansen girls who lived in the house at the head of the wharf. Her mother, Kathinka, was quite ill, she said, and she wanted Capi to get word out to the Columbia Coast Mission boat that would be passing by sometime in the early morning. The *Columbia* had a small hospital aboard, staffed with a nurse or doctor, and served as the lifeline of the coast. Could the *Caprice* run down Johnstone Strait to Salmon River (Kelsey Bay) where the store had a radio-telephone? Her mother was unwell a great deal of the time and often one of the children had to brave the strait to go down to the store and telegraph the *Columbia* for aid.

Capi woke the children and got the boat ready. They left at

4:00 A.M. when the tide was favourable. It can be a hard slog down to Kelsey Bay from Port Neville, but, luckily for everyone, it was a downwind run and Capi made the trip in about an hour. After anchoring the boat, she had to scramble up a muddy bank to the store: there was a wharf to tie up to but it was low tide, and the wharf was high and dry. She had to have the store owner, who was most likely Herbert Stanley Smith, contact the *Columbia* and relay the information about the emergency.

Serious illness or injury anywhere on the coast was always a major concern. Sometimes a sick person had to walk for miles and then row for days to get help or, if they were fortunate and another boat was around, they could avail themselves of the marine telegraph, as the Hansen girls did. Today, a few people still live in these outpost communities, but most have satellite phones and it only takes a seaplane, helicopter or fast vessel to get them to a hospital. Sometimes even pets use these services. When a beloved dog once needed emergency veterinary help, it was airlifted out of the back reaches of one of the archipelagos and flown across to Vancouver Island. The owner could not go with her dog so she secured a note to her collar that read, "I am very scared, please take good care of me, I am very nice but don't let me out near other dogs or I will bite them." A taxi driver was standing by to go to the vet as soon as the plane landed; the dog survived and lived a full life. While this may seem odd, it is part of the colour of the coast and an accepted way of life.

After their stay in Port Neville, when the *Caprice* turned northeast into the homelands of the Kwakwaka'wakw, where the rainforest reigns supreme, Capi and the children entered a maze of islands filled

with cul-de-sacs, dead ends and a confusing network of channels.[7] Getting lost is all too easy for the neophyte. A sheaf of charts, including both large and small scale, a copy of the *Sailing Directions, Volume 6*, of the *Canadian Tide and Current Tables* and a good tour book are essential. Even then, it is easy to get lost. Capi conceded this when she wrote, "As far as the eye could see, islands . . . crowded all round us . . . winding channels lured and beckoned . . . we were looking for old Indian villages, and we had to find out where we were. So we turned the chart this way and that way, trying to make it fit what lay before our eyes."[8]

The Kwakwaka'wakw are a water people who live along the northwest coast; it was the groups that inhabit the Broughton Archipelago that Capi wanted to see. Though it is not completely clear in *The Curve of Time* how many villages she and her children

visited, it is perhaps not important, as she was weaving a story and presenting images. Some of her accounts contain elements of several villages as if they were one, and the reader is left to tease out where she was and which group she was writing about. It is easy to see sameness in the artifacts of the past.

The houses in each of the villages were built side by side and near the beach, with boardwalks allowing easy access. Some houses had crests and supernatural creatures painted on the front. Canoes sat on the beaches under the shade of trees, to prevent them from cracking in the summer sun, and totem poles and welcome figures stood in front of the villages, telling their story and greeting visitors. Burial boxes were placed high up in the limbs of spruce trees or on slabs of wood on the ground on a small island or rock, not far from the village. There was a consistency among the villages, moulded by culture and environment. Yet there were variations between them, and too often, early accounts glossed over those differences. The Kwakwaka'wakw are not a unified group but instead live in communities loosely connected with each other through ancestry, language and tradition. Each tribe has its own creation story, chief, crest, lands, traditional clam beaches and eulachon fishing rights. There were eleven villages in the vicinity of Capi's travels, and she described four: the Mamalilikala of 'Mi'mkwamlis (Village Island), the Kwikwasutinexw at Gwa'yasdams (Gilford Island), the Lawitsis at Kalugwis (Turnour Island) and the 'Nakwaxda'xw at Ba'a's (Blunden Harbour).[9]

For Capi and the children, time ceased to exist once they entered the archipelago. They discovered remnants of the past existing side by side with viable working communities that appeared to slip in

Facing page: Aerial view of the Broughton Archipelago. COURTESY ROLF HICKER

and out of history with graceful ease. She referred to the Broughton as "this Land-of-the-Past . . . this forgotten land," because what she found were villages in a state of disrepair, some seemingly abandoned and others barely surviving.[10] Her reminiscences are important because she captured a people in transition. She wrote of seeing human bones and burial boxes, ceremonial spoons and bowls, weathered totems, no longer tall and straight but tilted and falling. She found a blend of twentieth-century clapboard houses and modern stoves alongside traditional longhouses and ringed stone firepits. In some villages she found only echoes of previous habitation and stumbled on fallen structures hidden by salal, salmonberry and thimbleberry shrubs. She met a man spear-fishing from his canoe and women sitting on a rocky knoll spinning nettle fibre and mountain goat wool. She wrote, "Yesterday, we . . . passed a slender Indian dugout. An Indian was standing . . . in the bow. Holding aloft a long fish-spear poised, ready to strike. His woman was crouched in the stern . . . When was it that we had watched them? Yesterday? A hundred years ago? Or just somewhere on that curve of time?"[11]

Facing page: Alert Bay. The residential school is the large building in the centre.

In Ba'a's Capi found a notice attached to a barred door that proclaimed, "Mr. Potladakami George. This chief of this Nagwadakwa People. It is get away. $265.00."[12] The village is gone now and the clam-shell beach empty of its harvesters, but at one end of the beach there is a small caretaker's hut, painted bright red, and a sign posted in the beach grass at the base of the stairs. It advises would-be tourists that the beach and upland area are private property, for this land still belongs to the 'Nakwaxda'xw.

The 19th- and 20th-century history of the Kwakwaka'wakw is

a sad mix of disease, misguided government policies and ideological clashes. Post-contact epidemics of smallpox, measles and tuberculosis ravaged villages, killing two-thirds of the people in this area.[13] Years of government pressure to abandon their language, their culture and their traditions interrupted their lives; the potlatch was banned, villages lost their teachers so children were relocated to Alert Bay to attend the residential school and communities were broken up. Villagers from Ba'a's in Blunden Harbour and Takus in Smith Inlet were sent to Port Hardy to live in a kind of cultural mishmash on someone else's land.

It is understandable that some of the villages looked abandoned when Capi visited. Indeed, even today, many people cruising in these waters assume the same and excitedly set their anchors to take a walk along the white shell beaches, poking into the remains of decaying houses or beating about in the bush looking for fallen totems, perhaps hoping to stand on that arc of time, to venture into the past. Despite appearances, however, these islands have not been abandoned. They remain traditional territories and demand respect. Many groups are in the process of cataloguing and studying their cultural heritage and some are resetting their villages.[14] The Da'naxda'xw from Tsadzis'nukwaame' (New Vancouver), for example, have returned to Dead Point on the north side of Harbledown Island and are now in the process of rebuilding and moving back to their village.[15]

It was dusk when the Blanchets dropped the anchor in Kalugwis (Karlukwees), on the southwest side of Turnour Island. They had been slowly working their way through Beware Passage and were skittish after having been blown the previous night out of Sunday Harbour—a small cove at the entrance to Arrow Passage that is open to westerly winds. Captain Daniel Pender named Beware Passage in 1869 after the HMS *Beware*. It is well named; the channel is littered with rocks. It looks as though the ancients were playing a game of giant jacks and left them where they fell for interlopers to stumble over. The *Sailing Directions* advise prudence when transitting this passage and suggest that it is best to navigate it at low water on a rising tide, when underwater dangers are visible.[16] The *Waggoner Cruising Guide* says, "Beware Passage will scare you to death."[17] Tired though they were, it was still a poor place to anchor, as a strong tidal current runs through the channel. Capi recognized this and wrote of the incident. "A swift tide thrummed its way through the massed kelp, and the eddies sucked and swirled over some hidden reef. If our boat sank in the night, it might be a couple of months before we were missed."[18]

Facing page: Coffin Island, near which Capi anchored, Kalugwis.

They could have spent the night in other coves. There is a snug little anchorage just across the channel in Potts Lagoon, but a logging operation was tied up there at the time. They were weary and really didn't want to go much farther; night was closing in around them and it would soon be too dark to see where they were going. Despite Capi's exhaustion from the previous night, sleep did not come to her, for a growing sense of unease crept into her thoughts. By day, K̲alugwis is a beautiful jewel, especially when the sun bounces off the white shell beach, brightening up everything in sight. But by night it can be a restless place, where nightmarish dreams mock rational thought. Perhaps it is the isolation and silence that play on the mind. Then, too, sleeping next to a sacred burial ground is disquieting. Almost within reaching distance of the boat were two islets where the Ławit̕sis buried their dead. To the visitor today, they look to be mere islets covered with a few scrubby trees, salal, moss and several varieties of grasses, but when Capi anchored next to them she saw burial boxes. Sitting prominently on one of the islets was a wolf crest painted on a nine-metre board and on the other was the crest of a killer whale. They were not alone.

The village of K̲alugwis is on a small piece of land, eleven hectares in size, that overlooks the junction of Clio Channel and Beware Passage. The crescent-shaped sand beach is one of the loveliest in the area. In fact, the very name "Qalogwis" means "bent beach" or "crooked beach."[19] The Ławitsis moved to K̲alugwis around 1850 from Klaoitsis, a small island in Clio Channel near West Cracroft Island. In 1886 it was designated as an Indian reserve, and by 1914 there was a small but thriving community consisting of twenty-one houses.[20] When Capi and the children arrived at the village, people were living there, although no one was around. Some of the villages

were inhabited only in winter. During the spring and summer months the people would leave their homes to fish or to work in the canneries that were scattered along the coast. Originally, <u>K</u>alugwis supported a few hundred people. When Capi visited, "whiteman" houses lined the beach, and all but one of the communal houses were gone.

Capi chose to ignore the clapboard houses in her discussions and focussed instead on the remaining historical artifacts. When they walked up the hill to the village, they were met by a number of totems standing in front. One large pole, carved by Charlie James, Mungo Martin's stepfather, was facing toward the sea, its base obscured by grass. Capi took one photograph of the framed structure of a cedar house showing two *huxwhukw*, or cannibal birds, with their long pointed beaks and outspread wings. The huxwhukw was said to be able to break open the skull of a human with its long beak and to eat the brains. Also among her photographs are two figures standing on each side of Chief Peter Smith's house. Where they once served as posts in the Big House they each now sported a large keg upon one shoulder. Capi did not mention these two posts in her book, perhaps because they seemed incongruous with what she had learned of totems and carving. Explaining the posts, Chief Peter Smith said, "After I built my whiteman style house, I put the old poles from my father's gukwdzi [Big House] alongside. I had to dig new holes and move the poles around so they faced the beach. Just for fun I put oak barrels on their shoulders where the house beams used to rest."[21]

Facing page: The crescent-shaped beach at <u>K</u>alugwis.

By 1974 only one of the posts was upright, and it had a gooseberry bush sprouting from its head. Some posts had become nurse logs for seedlings and homes for insects; others were stolen. Today there is one

house still standing, midway in the arc of the beach, its roofline and green dormer window visible to all who sail by. It is but a shell and is surrounded by bush so dense that only small birds and mice can wedge their way in. The Lawitsis have since scattered—the current population is approximately 107 people—and official government information lists the village as abandoned. While it is true that Ḵalugwis is no longer inhabited, the Lawitsis do visit from time to time and are actively involved in reaffirming their culture and history, as well as ensuring the continuity of their community.

Capi intended to go into Knight Inlet, but the wind was kicking up and it looked as though it might blow for days. While waiting for a turn in the weather she decided to visit 'Miʼmkwamlis (Village Island), which is seven kilometres north of Ḵalugwis. There are a few bays and coves on Village Island but the only real place to anchor is in Native Anchorage, which is where Capi went.[22] Native Anchorage offers good holding ground, but it is not well protected; it is exposed to both easterly and westerly winds, and when the wind funnels down through Canoe Passage, a narrow channel between Village Island and Turnour Island, it can set a boat twirling around in circles.

Facing page: The tall pole carved by Charlie James, at Ḵalugwis. Inset: Housepost that once belonged to the father of Chief Peter S. Smith, a huxwhukw holding a man, Ḵalugwis, 1935. This page: Figure beside Chief Peter Smith's house, Ḵalugwis.

PHOTOS BY CAPI BLANCHET, COURTESY JANET BLANCEHT

Village Island offered a cornucopia of experiences for Capi and

the children. There was a farm and a missionary settlement with a tuberculosis hospital, school and church. The western portion of the island was the traditional winter village of the Mamalilikala. The Oiens, an unlikely couple—he was Norwegian and she was Scottish—ran the farm and supplied the logging camps in the area with fresh fruit, vegetables, and dairy products provided by their two cows, one of which had an affinity for getting its foot caught in a bear trap. These cows deserve mention, as they were no ordinary cows. They were named Lucy and Mollie but were better known as public enemy numbers one and two for their penchant for wreaking havoc in the schoolroom and ripping clothing off the lines. They also helped themselves to cardboard boxes and ate them with apparent relish.

Facing page, top: The only house still standing at Kalugwis. Bottom: Dancer Randy Bell at Tśadzis'nukwaame', near Kalugwis. COURTESY ROLF HICKER

Besides having a good chat with Mrs. Oien, Capi and the children were able to replenish their stores and enjoy a delectable dish of fresh strawberries and cream—a rare extravagance in the wilderness. While visiting with the Oiens, Capi met Hughina Bowden, or Miss B, as she was called. Miss B was a young nurse and schoolteacher who came in 1935 to teach at the day school for two years. She lived with two missionary ladies who had been on the island for over thirty years, Kathleen O'Brien and Kate Dibben; Miss B referred to them as the GA's (guardian angels).

Miss O'Brien was an English lady who had left the tea parties of British society for a life of missionary work among the First Nations on the BC coast. She built a small sanatorium in 'Mi'mkwamlis in 1900 and, with her friend Miss Dibben, ministered to the children who had contracted tuberculosis or other "whiteman's" diseases. Later, a church and a schoolhouse were built, the latter easily identified by the Union Jack that sat atop it. It is almost certain that Capi met them, but she did not refer to either of them by name. Miss O'Brien was very friendly but hard of hearing. She used an ear trumpet, the effectiveness of which depended on how loud one was willing to shout into it. Miss Dibben, the more unbending of the two, suffered from glaucoma and had only partial sight left in one eye. They lived in a cold, draughty float home that sat on a raft; its windows and doors never really fit as a result of the constant movement of the water. O'Brien and Dibben continued their missionary work until their retirement in 1945. After spending more than half their lives on the West Coast, they both went back to England. Kathleen O'Brien remained there, obtained recognition on the King's Honours List and was awarded membership in the Order of the British Empire for her work at 'Mi'mkwamlis. Kate Dibben returned to BC and lived out the remainder of her life in Alert Bay. Hughina Harold (née Bowden) wrote a delightful book, *Totem Poles and Tea*, about Dibben's experiences at 'Mi'mkwamlis.

When Capi visited in the 1930s there were about a hundred people living at 'Mi'mkwamlis, but she did not mention seeing anyone other than the Oiens and the missionary women. It is most likely that many of the residents were away, fishing or working at their summer jobs. Life was demanding and full, but in the mid-1940s things began to change. The children on the island were left without a teacher, and the residents had no medical support. Many villagers left and moved to Alert Bay. By the late 1960s the village was empty and most of the houses had been vandalized: bed frames rusted on the beach; doors were missing

Facing page: Storage shed on the beach at 'M'imkwamlis.

from their hinges; windows were broken; insulation hung from the ceilings and fell in great wet lumps onto piles of clothing; and broken dishes were scattered on the floors.

Today there are still a few reminders of the past. Two house posts that framed the entrance to the Big House are fixed solidly in the ground, and a few of the clapboard houses are still standing. The hospital, however, is collapsing on itself. Where once it was bright and cheery, it is now eerily dark and mosquito-infested, as the forest slinks through the windows. Totem poles have given way to tall grasses, blackberry bushes and honeysuckle vines, but the remnants of a cedar-carved sea lion can be found in the grass near where the Big House once stood. At the south end of the village there was a twelve-metre totem pole that featured an eagle, a killer whale, a raven, a sea wolf, a bear and a human on its frame. It did not have an owner so it was moved, periodically, until it came to its final resting place at the edge of the village. It stood for many years, perhaps

seventy or so, and was the last pole left until it too succumbed to age and toppled onto the forest floor.

Although Capi toured 'Mi'mkwamlis she did not write much about the village, once one of the largest on the coast, covering 178 hectares. It was also where the government and First Nations met head-on in a final, crushing blow to potlatching.

In December 1921 Chief Dan Cranmer hosted a large potlatch that had taken seventeen years of planning and preparation. By having the potlatch at 'Mi'mkwamlis, Chief Cranmer hoped to avoid notice, but Indian Agent Halliday knew of it and arrested forty-five people.[23] They were charged with making speeches, dancing and gift-giving, and were taken to Alert Bay where they awaited trial. The defence attorney pleaded for leniency of the court; twenty were sent to Oakalla Prison in Burnaby, 448 kilometres away. Potlatching simply went deeper underground and operated under the guise of small house parties, but Chief Dan Cranmer's potlatch was the last of its kind until thirty-one years later, when Chief Mungo Martin held the first public potlatch in Victoria in 1952.

'Mi'mkwamlis continued to be a staging ground for clashes between differing ideologies. In the 1940s it was the first village in the immediate area to have an electric-light plant; a five-h.p. engine and a five-kilowatt generator provided electricity to eight houses. Plans were drafted for a fish-processing plant, and new houses with modern conveniences were being built. To "whiteman's" ways of thinking, this was progress—assimilation at last. But such changes brought conflict among the residents and some eventually left 'Mi'mkwamlis.[24] It is

Facing page, top: Houses still standing at 'Mi'mkwamlis. Bottom: The totem pole that was moved periodically at 'Mi'mkwamlis, still standing in 1989.

not that such conveniences were not desired; it was more that cultural transformations were happening too quickly. Telescoping time into one dimension may have appealed to Maeterlinck but it does not work in all situations. The present needed time to develop into the future.

'Mi'mkwamlis is now empty of human habitation; fifty-one people live on other reserves, another 329 have scattered to cities and small communities. It is a destination for kayakers and cruisers. They come to walk upon the grassy fields, hoping to catch an image or impression of the ancient stories, the dancing and gift-giving that once took place in the big plank house that overlooked Eliot Passage.

Capi's most vivid descriptions were of Gwa'yasdams (Health Bay on Gilford Island). She took quite a number of photographs of the village, and her knowledge of and keen interest in First Nations cultures were evident in her descriptions. Gwa'yasdams is home to the Kwikwasutinexw. Historically, it was a winter village where people gathered for their ceremonials. In 1856 the Bella Coola people massacred all but twelve of the people living at Gwa'yasdams, and then in 1862 smallpox swept through the area. The survivors moved to 'Mi'mkwamlis, Tsaxis at Fort Rupert or Okwunalis at the mouth of the Kingcome River. Some returned to Gwa'yasdams in the 1890s. In 1991 there were forty-one residents in the village, but five years later the number dropped to twenty-eight. However, as 2006 neared its end, the population had increased to forty-four.

Even though Gwa'yasdams is deep inside the archipelago, it is impossible to miss. Gilford Island is one of the larger islands in the Broughton; it has a water aerodrome (a stretch of water designated by Transport Canada where floatplanes land and take off) and planes can often be seen coming and going in Health Bay. In addition, there is a magnetic anomaly in Retreat Passage; errors up to 18° can occur, so as a vessel approaches the vicinity of Meade Bay, a stone's throw from Gwa'yasdams, the compass runs amok. When one is abeam of Health Bay, the uniformity of the horizon is unexpectedly interrupted by a delightful collage of colour, for, at the head of the lagoon, the houses are painted royal blue, yellow, green, turquoise and white, some two-toned, others not. There are also magnificent greeting totems at the head of the dock, carved by Sam Johnson, a very talented artist. It is a treat for the senses.

In November 2005 Gwa'yasdams became front-page news. The community had been under a boil-water advisory for nine years, the sewage system had failed, there was saltwater in the freshwater system and all twenty-six homes had serious mould problems. The mould was so obvious that large black rings, which looked distinctly like horizontal cross-sections of trees, covered the walls of the houses. The people had a continuous string of respiratory problems, chest infections, skin rashes and ear infections. Finally, in 2005 the government promised to build a new water system and to replace all the houses. The residents of the village moved out of their homes in 2007 while construction crews demolished the old houses and rebuilt new ones.

Unfortunately, substandard living conditions are not the only problem the Kwikwasutinexw have had to deal with. They are also losing access to their traditional food stocks—salmon, clams, prawns and crabs—due to the destruction of their habitat caused by human encroachment and the increasing frequency of natural disasters, as well as disease, sea lice and effluent from nearby fish farms. They say that many of their traditional clams beds are now polluted and that 95 per cent of certain species of young wild salmon stocks have been lost. What the future holds is unknown, but the Kwikwasutinexw are fighting to maintain their way of life and hope to be able to raise their children and children's children on the traditional land of their ancestors.

During an earlier time, Emily Carr brought Gwa'yasdams to the attention of the public with her painting of dzunukwa (dzo'noq!wa).[25] Her introduction to dzunukwa was by way of a slug. While visiting Gwa'yasdams Carr slipped on the sticky slime left by the ubiquitous Pacific banana slugs and fell headlong into a patch of stinging nettles. "The shock on picking oneself out of this predicament to come face to face with the Spirit of the Woods with its outstretched arms and diabolical face. But there she stands towering above the nettles; we reached a little above her knee as we stood beside her."[26] Dzunukwa stood tall, reaching a height of six metres. She is a mythical character sometimes termed the "Lady Giant" or "Wild Woman of the Woods." She was fearsome, with her long, red-painted body and huge, black

head, heavy brow and protruding lips. Her cheeks and eyes were sunken, giving her a cadaverous appearance. Dzunukwa is always shown with heavy eyebrows and deep-set, half-closed eyes. The accepted description is that it makes her sleepy-looking. She was said to run through the forest collecting children to take them home to eat, but she was also the bringer of wealth and fortune for those who could outsmart her.

When Capi dropped anchor at Gwa'yasdams the first thing she mentioned was meeting dzunukwa. "A great black wooden figure, standing waist high in the nettles up on the bank, welcomed us with outstretched arms . . . I looked at the huge figure with the fallen breasts, the pursed-out lips, the greedy arms. It was Dsonoqua."[27] Young David was wary of this giant denizen of the forest and kept far away from the reaches of her arms, lest

she eat him, too. Before Capi's visit, dzunuḵwa once had coppers in each hand and one above her head, which signalled the payment of a marriage debt. The only parts left of the original carving are sections of her head, currently housed in the Burke Museum of Natural History and Culture in Seattle, Washington. Fortunately, the museum had a replica carved, which is displayed at the entrance to the museum.

From the beach Capi walked up the steep wooden steps that led to the village. Stretched out before her was a plank boardwalk that ran the length of the entire village. At Gwa'yasdạms she was presented with an intermingling of the old and the new, and once again she focussed her photographs and discussion solely on the traditional. The houses that Capi saw were giving way to nettles and wild parsnips. The longitudinal beams and carved crossbeams outlined what was left of some of the longhouses, but the roofs and walls had fallen and lay in the underbrush. Describing one of the Big Houses she wrote, "Its main uprights or house posts were two great wooden ravens [they were actually huxwhukw] with outstretched wings. Fourteen feet high, wing tip touching wing tip, great beaks and fierce eyes . . . stared across to where, some sixty feet away, a couple of killer whales standing on their tails formed a companion pair of posts."[28]

Towering over the village was a striking pole that sat beside Chief Johnny Scow's Raven House.[29] The totem was carved by Mungo

Martin, one of the most significant of the northwest coast artists. This was the second pole he carved, and it featured Scow's principal crests. It showed a whale, with the ancestor who had harpooned the great whale placed near the top of the pole, just under a flying thunderbird; under the whale's flukes was a raven. The pole captured the attention of Emily Carr and was featured in *Old Indian House*, an oil-on-canvas painting she did in 1912. In Carr's painting the pole is in front of the house where the whale's mouth served as part of the entryway. In 1915 Chief Scow, by then a widower, married a noble Heiltseuk woman and the pole was moved to the side of the house, which is where Capi saw it.

At the far end of the village and up a knoll, where the forest grew dense, was the burial site for the community. When people died they were arranged in the fetal position, wrapped in a cedar mat, and placed in a cedar box. The box was then lashed onto a wooden plank and set high up in a tree or laid in a tomb built of wood and placed on a small island or rocky outcropping near the village. Many visitors, impressed by the burial trees, have photographed and written of the great cedar and spruce that held the deceased. The Barrows, for example, on their visit to Gwa'yasdams in 1936, noted that the burial boxes "are about 20 to 30 feet up the trees and some are higher up

Facing page: Huxwhukw houseposts, Gwa'yasdams. PHOTO BY CAPI BLANCHET, COURTESY JANET BLANCHET

still. A cedar-board above and below the coffin box. In some of the trees there are three or four coffin boxes, on branches one below the other."[30] Jim Spilsbury, a mid-twentieth-century pioneer, aviator and writer about the BC coast, described the extent of the burial trees. "Some places were absolutely littered with dead Indians . . . Cedar boards and skulls were scattered through the bush. Fallers at one of the camps said you couldn't stick an axe in a tree without a bunch of bones coming down on your head."[31]

Capi was more anthropological in her discussions of burial trees, writing of the techniques used to make the cedar boxes and the history of burial practices. At Gwa'yasdams she stumbled on the burial trees quite by accident. She was walking on the mud flats toward the end of the village and stepped on a bracelet of twisted copper. She bent down and picked it up, later estimating that the bracelet was about 150 years old. "Personal items like that would have been buried with their owners," she wrote. "Suddenly I remembered the old tree-burials, and glanced above my head at the great trees that overhung the water. There . . . swaying in the breeze, hung long strands of cedar bark rope that had once bound a box-of-the-dead to the upper branches."[32]

It is hard to say if Capi was particularly sensitive to the nuances of coastal cultures; she certainly did her homework and was well read on some of the more visible traditions and cultural practices of

the people she visited. She did not seem to be caught up in 1930s paternalism and stereotypical notions of "place," but she did talk of First Nations groups in the objective, as if they somehow existed outside of or were peripheral to her world view. While she carefully described many of the artifacts she found, she ignored their ownership. For example, she picked up a spinning whorl that was being used by a group of women, ignoring their presence, and she mentioned that her children played in some of the boxes of the dead, disregarding their sanctity. She inferred a lack of concern and care on the part of the villagers for leaving the boxes and artifacts about. The Barrows implied the same: "I expect a lot of good stuff has been looted as Indians are always careless in leaving everything laying about."[33] Capi did take home a few of the artifacts she found—an empty burial box, which she kept in her kitchen, and a number of bracelets, one of which she wore for years. In Ba'a's she removed two ceremonial ladles to take back to the *Caprice* to photograph. Whether she returned them to the village is not known, but she did not take them with her. In the main, Capi left most artifacts where she found them.

Facing page, top: Burial box, Gwa'yasdams. Bottom: Chief Johnny Scow's totem pole, carved by Mungo Martin, Gwa'yasdams. PHOTO BY CAPI BLANCHET, COURTESY JANET BLANCHET

For years people have been combing the beaches, taking off trade beads, pottery and carvings, slowly stripping ancestral villages of their material heritage. There are now legal protections against the removal of indigenous property, but in Capi's time no such regulations existed and cultural sensitivities were discounted. The destruction of ancient burial sites, primarily by unregulated land-use development, is an ongoing issue and has yet to be resolved.

Capi's last stop on her tour of First Nations villages was at Ba'a's in

Blunden Harbour, on the mainland side of Queen Charlotte Strait. Getting to Blunden Harbour is always a challenge. One can either follow the shoreline from Wells Passage, as Capi did, or cross Queen Charlotte Strait from the Vancouver Island side. It is a region of intense storms, which hit the area every two to three days in the winter months. In the summer months, when the warmer Pacific air moves over the colder water, dense sea fog can form without warning, swallowing up boats and muting sound. It can be disorienting and dangerous, but travel here can be as thrilling as it is harrowing. The scenery is majestic, raw and wild. Stunted, wind-swept trees hug the edges of sun-bleached cliffs, and granite monoliths form treeless islands that tell of a time before man. It is a place rich with marine life; rock-strewn islands with great green tufts of grass act as nesting sites for over 600,000 sea birds. There are orcas, humpbacks, minke and grey whales, as well as a large breeding rookery of Steller's sea lions. Dolphins and porpoises are almost always about, often challenging passing boats to a game of catch-me-if-you-can, as they shoot through the water like torpedoes, flashing back and forth just centimetres under the bow.

Facing page: Ba'a's welcome figures along boat dock, 1901.

COURTESY BC ARCHIVES

Blunden Harbour is a secluded spot with a well-protected bay; its entrance is hidden by Robinson Island, which has no distinguishing features. There is a speck of an islet, Burgess Island, about half a kilometre southwest of the entrance that provides identification of the way in. Care needs to be taken to avoid several hazards: Siwiti Rock, near the entrance, has less than two metres of water over it, and there are rocks along both sides of the passage into the inner harbour, between the Augustine Islands and Robinson Island.

In 1918 Blunden Harbour was home to a number of settlers, or

pre-emptors, who tried their luck at homesteading. Under the Land Ordinance of 1870, settlers could hold partially surveyed Crown land under temporary title for the purposes of building a homestead or for agriculture. They settled in an area called Port Progress, opposite Jula Island and the Frost Islands at the north end of the eastern arm of the bay. They had to clear the land, build their houses and wrest arable soil from the forest. They grew vegetables, harvesting turnips and cabbages the size of bowling balls; they raised chickens, goats and rabbits, and a few turned their talents to distilling liquor. Their houses were well built; they had a type of rain-screen system, shingle and shake exteriors and large glass windows. There were actually several homesteads spread between Kenneth Bay and Blunden Harbour, a distance of about eighteen kilometres. To connect their properties, the pre-emptors built a trail along the coastline. They had picnics and social gatherings, even bringing their dogs with them, but life was hard.

They were extremely isolated on an inhospitable part of the coast, the winters were rough and their only mode of transportation was rowboats or small skiffs, which they had to depend on to get them across the strait to Port Hardy for their supplies. It is not surprising that they eventually gave up and moved on. In the 1920s and 30s there was a logging operation farther up the inlet, in Bradley Lagoon. Billy Proctor, a long-time resident of the Broughton Archipelago, said that a group of Japanese workers moved into the lagoon to work as loggers, living in primitive conditions. "Their houses," he said, "were pulled-up floats at the end of the long wide arm of the lagoon."[34]

Facing page: Joan with wooden spoon or ladle, Ba'a's. PHOTO BY CAPI BLANCHET, COURTESY JANET BLANCHET

Ba'a's was the winter home of the 'Nakwaxda'xw.[35] Capi found no one at home, but the village was actively occupied. The houses were carved out of the forest and positioned in a linear fashion along the beach. In front of the houses was the usual hand-hewn cedar boardwalk, supported by a log dyke. During times of high tide the stairs leading from the houses to the beach were partially submerged. The 'Nakwaxda'xw were harvesters of the sea, as well as hunters and trappers; they had approximately 130 hectares of intertidal clam beds, over 400 hectares of kelp beds, a wealth of abalone and plenty of rockfish.[36] Had anyone been home at the time Capi visited, she might have found the women collecting clams from the bay in front of their village and drying seaweed in large sheets, preserving this bounty for the coming winter. When she walked through the village there were two traditional community houses left. Inside one of them were some

of the most beautiful masks and ritual paraphernalia that she had seen. What she found were most likely items made by Willie Seaweed, a master carver and sculptor of international repute.[37] She took several photographs at Ba'a's, including one of a large carved wooden spoon or ladle that looks to be about 1.5 metres in length. The handle was a raven, with its beak folded down, lying along the front of its body, and its wings pressed tightly against its sides. Capi also photographed the bottom of another ladle that was carved in the shape of a face, with eyes, nose and protruding mouth and teeth.

Outside, at the back of the house, Capi came face-to-face with a *sisiyutl* board, which stood upright in the bushes. The sisiyutl was a scaly, double-headed serpent with horns and a long protruding tongue. In the centre of its body was a human face with horns and bared teeth. The sisiyutl was a shape-shifter and could appear as a fish or a self-propelled canoe. It was reported to bring death to any human who caught sight of it or great power to those who learned

how to harness it. The Blanchet children found the village dark and frightening and told their mother they wanted to leave. As they rowed their dinghy back to the *Caprice*, a state of apprehension lay heavily on the little boat and its passengers.

Leaving the bay, they passed a small round islet on their right side. It was Byrnes Island, the burial site for the village. In her description Capi wrote, "We passed close to the burial island. It was very overgrown, but above the nettles and the salmonberry bushes the two heads of a great sisciatl [sisiyutl] dared us to touch the dead of their tribe."[38] Byrnes Island looks like an insignificant rock that is covered by tall trees, where eagles sometimes perch on outstretched branches, but a sense of spirit whistles through the trees.

Facing page: A modern sisiyutl in Alert Bay. This page: Byrnes Island, the burial island in Blunden Harbour.

There is a story about an island, perhaps Byrnes, and how the people came to Ba'a's. "About the year 1894, the head chief and a party were hunting at Paás (Blunden Harbour), when his son fell ill, and, about to die, begged them: 'Do not bury me at Téquhsta, for there they eat the dead. Bury me here.' So they placed his body on a small island, and the chief told the people that he would remain there until he died. But rather than give up their chief, the people left Téquhsta and went to Paás, where they have since maintained their winter residence."[39] Ba'a's became the principal winter residence site in 1894 when the 'Nakwaxda'xw moved, probably from Kequesta, which is north of Ba'a's at Point Nugent in Nugent Sound. Several places served as old village sites, so it is not possible to be completely accurate. Ba'a's was the subject of a painting by Emily Carr, titled *Blunden Harbour*, which is in the National Gallery in Ottawa. The village was also used as the location of Edward Curtis's 1914 film *In the Land of the War Canoes*.[40]

The 'Nakwaxda'xw lived at Ba'a's until 1964, when they were relocated to Port Hardy by the Department of Indian Affairs on the theory that it would be cheaper and more convenient to provide services from a centralized station. The government held token consultations with the 'Nakwaxda'xw and promised them improved housing, schools and services, as well as increased employment opportunities. To assure compliance, the DIA threatened to eliminate all funding to Ba'a's unless they agreed to the move. The relocation was a monumental failure. The promised housing was not provided; social services were unavailable; the people suffered culture shock and experienced racism; and the Kwagu'ł, on whose land they were resettled, resented them. Infant mortality for the first decade rose to 18 per cent, and many of the children spent years in the social welfare system, living in foster homes or adopted by non-Aboriginal families, and the death rate for seniors, for the first few years after relocation, was double that of their age cohort.[41] The rhythm of their community was fractured, culture cohesiveness thrown on the pyre of government paternalism and expediency.

Photographs taken of Ba'a's in 1967 spoke volumes about the state of the people. Windows were broken, iron headboards lay rusting against walls that were overtaken by vines, empty cardboard boxes sat on the floors, dishes and suitcases were strewn about—the past was gone. Today the beach is empty except for a caretaker's hut. It is a presence, a reminder that this is the village of the 'Nakwaxda'x̱w, once the home of great carvers and experienced sea-people.

Capi and the children had been waiting out the windy weather at 'Mi'mkw̲amlis and were anxious to get moving when some friends came alongside the *Caprice* and invited them aboard their ketch for a trip to the head of Knight Inlet. It would have been an uncomfortable venture for the *Caprice*, and Capi felt that a sailboat would ride the weather more smoothly. Knight Inlet is a deeply cut gorge, a mile and a half in width, bounded by towering mountains averaging 1,700 metres in height. With depths ranging anywhere from seventy to over three hundred metres, the inlet has few good anchorages. At about one hundred kilometres, from Wedge Island, at the eastern entrance to Dutchman Head at the upper end, Knight Inlet is the longest fjord on the BC coast. For a boat like the *Caprice*, or a sailing vessel that travels 5 or 6 knots, the trip can take anywhere from eleven to thirteen hours.

It was a good opportunity for the Blanchets to explore Knight Inlet. Their friends had a package to deliver to the Stantons, a couple who lived at the top of the inlet where the Klinaklini and Franklin rivers meet at Dutchman Head. The wind was freshening, and with

every curve in the mountains or dip in a valley it funnelled down and hit them beam on, causing the mainsail to jibe across the boat. Capi wrote, "We would no sooner get it settled . . . when 'wha-a-am' back it would go again."[42] At the same time they were struggling with a beam sea, in which the waves come at right angles to the direction of the boat. The farther into the inlet they sailed, the higher the mountains became, hiding all that existed behind them. The "mountains grew higher and higher, and gossiped together across our heads," Capi wrote. "And somewhere down at their feet, on that narrow ribbon of water, our boat with the white sails flew swiftly along, completely dwarfed by its surroundings."[43]

This page: Caretaker's hut, Ba'a's. Facing page: Knight Inlet. COURTESY ROLF HICKER

Capi said she had never felt so small or inconsequential anywhere on the coast as she did in Knight Inlet. It took them three days to reach their destination.

For well over a hundred years Knight Inlet has been subject to logging activity; today there are several dryland sorts and booming operations, as well as heli-logging. When Capi travelled up Knight they had four lookouts on the bow, watching for deadheads—logs that float vertically, with their tops just under the water. "We could see nothing much below the surface of the water," she wrote, "and when the lookout in the bow called out 'Deadhead!' we had to slow to a crawl . . . This last reach was full of them . . . with great stumps that floated with their roots all spread out like tentacles."[44] Sometimes the only visual clue to a deadhead is a small, nearly imperceptible smooth patch of water outlining the top of the log. It is not much to go on, especially in murky water and choppy seas.

One of the old monarchs of the coast, the *Blue Fjord*, a wooden-hulled, nineteen-metre vessel built in 1931, once a provincial police floating courthouse that served the coast between Victoria, Prince

Rupert and the Queen Charlotte Islands, hit a submerged log in 2005 and sank.[45] Referring to the incident, the owner said, "I heard a horrendous crunch. The impact almost stopped the 50-tonne boat. It was a hemlock log. I saw it on impact, it spun and sank again and I never saw it again."[46] It was a tragedy but not an uncommon story.

By the time the sailboat reached Glendale Cove, a run of about sixty kilometres from 'Mi'mkwa̱mlis, everybody felt a little queasy. The cove offers calmer waters and protection from the wind, a good antidote for seasickness, and has become world famous as a place to witness bears in their natural habitat. Glendale estuary has the highest concentration of grizzlies along the coast. During the spring and fall, dozens of bears can be seen cavorting in the shallows, turning over rocks and picking at the chitons or isopods.

While Capi made no mention of bears in Glendale Cove, she did note the cannery that was at the head of it. A fish packer had just come

in with a load of fish when she was there, and everyone aboard the ketch was invited to see first-hand how the processing plant operated. Capi wrote, "We watched the fish leap from the packer onto the endless belt, onto the moving tables where the Indian women waited with sharp knives, and then into the tins, in an unbelievably short time. So fast that you still seemed to sense some life in the labelled tins."[47]

Facing page: The *Blue Fjord*.

The cannery was the Anglo-British Columbia Packing Company, known as the ABC Packing Company, the world's largest producer of tinned sockeye salmon. It was an old company, established in 1891 by Henry Ogle Bell-Irving who became an influential Vancouver businessman and industrialist. The company started with nine fish canneries and slowly expanded over the years, continuing until 1974, when it folded. According to Billy Proctor, ABC moved to Glendale Cove in 1915 and stayed in operation until 1950. The company kept a watchman at the cannery until, in 1967, it burned down.[48]

There is little sign, today, of the cannery, store and logging operation that once made the cove a bustling centre for Knight Inlet. A few rotting pilings that used to support a jetty remain, but that is all. Tucked into Glendale Cove is Knight Inlet Lodge, a floating resort that takes guests to see the grizzlies at the mud flats at the head of the bay; 2,300 visitors from nineteen countries come to visit the bears every year.[49] The owners, Dean and Kathy Wyatt, were pioneers in wilderness-based bear viewing and have worked diligently in the area of grizzly bear conservation and salmon stewardship programs for Knight Inlet and the Broughton Archipelago.[50]

On day three of their trip Capi and her friends pulled into Dutchman Head to drop off the parcel for the Stantons. They found it impossible to anchor; they were in either twenty-four metres of water or ashore—there was no middle ground—so they eventually tied up to a deadhead that Capi said seemed "fairly stationary." Jim and Laurette Stanton had been living in Knight Inlet since 1919 and, except for one brief stay in Victoria when his wife died, Jim lived there off and on until 1978 when he passed away at the ripe old age of ninety-three. Dutchman Head may be in a remote area and hard to get to but the Stantons had plenty of visitors during the summer months. Cruisers loved visiting with Jim and Laurette and watching the grizzlies on the flats at the mouth of the Klinaklini River. Jim was in the guiding business and would take fishermen, hunters and climbers up the Klinaklini or the Franklin and into the mountains beyond. Dutchman Head provides access to some of BC's highest mountains: Mount Waddington, for example, stands at 4,019 metres and is the highest peak in the Coast Range. Every summer Jim helped Don and Phyllis Munday, Canada's premiere mountain climbers in the 1920s and 30s, pack their equipment across the Franklin Glacier and to their base camp.

The mud flats next to Dutchman Head are prime grounds for bears; every summer hundreds of them come down to feast on salmon. Capi, always protective of her children, was somewhat nervous about bears. During her visit with the Stantons she learned that the flats the children were playing on were usually visited by a number of bears that came down looking for their supper in the late afternoon. The mere thought of bears sent her heart racing. She had already rescued her children a few times from bear encounters and had no wish to endanger them further. She looked at her watch and noticed it was 3:30. Is this the time the bears came down, she wondered? She had learned to trust her instincts where the children were concerned, so she left what she was doing and ran as fast as she could to the dinghy.

With images of her children and bears swimming in her thoughts, she rowed frantically to the flats, all the while yelling for their attention. She had been told by Jim not to worry, the children would be fine; the bears did not usually attack men. "Just when did a grizzly consider that a boy had reached man's estate?" she wanted to know.[51] And if they were due at the flats at 4:00 P.M., was it the same 4:00 P.M. every day or "did it just depend on when the bears felt four-o-clockish, and simply had to have their tea?"[52] When she reached the flats, she gathered the children together, piled them into the boat and rowed away as quickly as she could. Just as they got back to the boat, five big bears came ambling out, sniffing where the children had just been and looking about for the intruders.

Knight Inlet is at the southern end of what has become known as the Great Bear Rainforest, a term coined by Ian and Karen McAllister, two conservationists who in the 1990s filmed, photographed and wrote about bears in the northern raincoast ecology.[53] The Great Bear Rainforest covers 64,000 square kilometres, stretching from Knight Inlet to the border of Alaska, and is part of a very rare and increasingly diminished coastal temperate rainforest system. Over 60 per cent of the world's temperate rainforests have disappeared as a direct result of human activity. The Great Bear Rainforest has some of the largest trees on the planet and is home to one of the densest populations of grizzly bears in North America. Many groups have taken on the job of trying to protect this area, and in January 2007, the federal government, provincial government, forest industry and private groups announced the groundbreaking Great Bear Rainforest Agreement that will aid its conservation. The agreement will protect over 2 million hectares from logging, and 7 million hectares will operate under an ecologically sustainable management system, though the protected areas are scattered, not contiguous, and form only part of this crucial ecosystem.[54]

Capi did not mention the reserve, across the estuary from Dutchman Head. Perhaps she did not know of it; she only spent an afternoon there. Historically, Dzawadi (Knight Inlet) was home to the Dạ'naxdạ'x̱w, but sometime in 1840 or 1850 the Bella Coola, Chilcotin and Carrier slaughtered many of them for transgressions that had occurred between the Dạ'naxdạ'x̱w and the Bella Coola.[55] Dzawadi was one of the traditional eulachon-harvesting areas and Kwakwaka'wakw families return annually to fish the eulachon for their oil or t'lina (pronounced "gleetna"), an important food staple rich in vitamins and minerals. It takes about three weeks to render oil from the eulachon, a time-consuming and smelly process.[56] In addition to being valuable as a food and for its medicinal properties, t'lina was historically viewed as a sign of wealth. It was traded commercially,

and to receive bottles of t'lina as a gift during a potlatch ceremony was a great honour.

It is impossible to spend any time cruising along the coast without being affected by the experience. Lazy summers surrounded by the towering trees, high cliffs and fjords of the rainforest, moving among the marine life, marking its habits and rhythms in a life dictated by the weather and tides, alter a person's sense of self and place in the world. Bravado and machismo have no status in this environment. Cruising teaches humility, and the elements caution against impatience and flippancy. This makes some people a little less anxious, more peaceful, less needful of urban trappings and large groups. It made Capi and her children stronger, more self-sufficient and less tolerant of artificial conventions. But Capi's children grew up and went off on their own ventures; the last of her cruising photographs are dated around 1937. By then Elizabeth was twenty-four, Frances twenty-three, Joan twenty-one, Peter eighteen and David thirteen years of age. The long summer cruises aboard the *Caprice* had ended.

Facing page: Orcas, an important part of marine life along the coast.

CHAPTER FIVE ✤

Life after the *Caprice*

By 1939 war was being waged in Europe, and Canada began mobilizing its militia in response. The coast suddenly took on a different aspect and, except for those who volunteered to work through the newly established Power Boat Squadron to patrol the coast, pleasure cruising basically stopped. There were fears that Victoria and Vancouver could be hit by incendiary bombs and razed, and it was important to clear the coast of all unnecessary craft. Gas was rationed and pleasure boaters were allowed only enough to run their boats for about an hour a month, which was not enough to take anyone far afield.

Canada began shoring up its coastal defences: artillery batteries were set up at Esquimalt, Jordan River, Otter Point, Patricia Bay, Ucluelet, Tofino, Port Hardy and Coal Harbour. Yorke Island, at the junction of Sunderland Channel and Race Passage in Johnstone Strait, protected the Inside Passage with two forty-millimetre Bofors AA guns. Partway up the hill, on the southwest side of the island, remnants of the military installation can still be seen. Commercial ships continued to traverse the waters but were subject to strict regulations governing blackouts. Darkness makes it hard for an enemy to spot a potential target but also makes it difficult for ships in transit to see the coastline. To warn ships of impending danger, the

Facing page: Capi.
COURTESY JANET BLANCHET

first few bars of "The Road to Mandalay" were played over the radio. This meant all lights out—immediately—lighthouses, as well as ships' navigation lights. During one such alert a troop carrier coming down Queen Charlotte Strait ran aground off Pulteney Point Lighthouse. There is a story about an old-time fisherman who was running past Yorke Island and failed to heed the warning tune; he cruised right on by with all of his navigation lights on. He survived the volley of ammunition that peppered the strait, but it sent an instant message to the rest of the fishing fleet—Canada was serious about protecting its shores.

Capi kept the *Caprice* until after the war, when she sold it for a hundred dollars more than its original price. Parting with a boat that has been so much a part of one's life can be stressful. It signals a transitioning in life's process—leaving one stage behind and taking up another. Capi was a no-nonsense sort of person and would probably have simply "got on with it." Unfortunately, the *Caprice* met its end shortly after she sold it. It was up on a marine ways in Victoria when the entire boatyard went up in flames, the *Caprice* along with it. It was a sad ending for the little boat that had carried its passengers along the coast so reliably for twelve years.

Capi had a new boat built and christened it *Scylla*. In Greek mythology, *Scylla* was a six-headed creature that guarded Cape Skilla in northwest Greece and would devour mariners alive if they sailed too close. Capi's *Scylla* was a little less frightening. It was a six-metre, clinker-built day cruiser powered by a Grey Marine engine. Dick Johnson, who had a boatshed and marine railway a little south of Canoe Cove, built the hull, and Capi did some of the finishing work herself, with the help of David. The *Scylla* was adorned with teak trim that required concentrated attention; sometimes tempers would flare with Capi and David shouting at each other but only when they thought no one else was within earshot. While they never blasphemed, "You poor fool" was volleyed across the hull during one intense session of copper riveting. It was the most degrading of insults for the Blanchets.

When the *Scylla* was completed Capi moored it at a modest marina in Canoe Cove, just down the lane from her house. Hugh Rodd, who, in 1935, built an attractive stone house that became his residence, ran the marina. The house was referred to as The Landing, but today it is a popular restaurant and pub called The Stonehouse Pub. It still has the original hand-hewed beams, as well as the fir floors and leaded windows, but the Canoe Cove that Capi knew is significantly changed. Canoe Cove Marina has become one of the largest marinas and repair yards for pleasure boats in British Columbia.

The *Scylla* never travelled the path that the *Caprice* did. Capi took it out for short jaunts around the Gulf Islands and once ventured as far as the mainland, but she never repeated her earlier summer excursions along the coast.[1] David and his wife, Janet, sometimes used it to cruise around the Gulf Islands for a week or so at a time. The *Scylla* was still in Capi's possession when she died; it was about eight years old at the time and was assessed at $1,250.

Capi, of course, did still live by the sea, so her activities were coloured by her sea-going attitudes. Sometimes when she cooked fish she put the dirty dishes at the water's edge for the ocean to clean. Janet tells of a time Capi took her dishes down when the tide was out. She left them by a tree, intending to go back at high water, but she got sidetracked and forgot about them for a couple of days. When she returned, the dishes were missing. She was so angry that she drove into Sidney to put a notice in the local newspaper. It read, "Would the person seen taking plates and silver from Curteis Point please return them."[2] In fact, the cove could not be seen from Capi's house—she was going after effect more than anything. Shortly thereafter she noticed a fishboat circling around in the cove, looking quite suspicious. By the time she got down to the beach to see what was going on, the boat had left, but next to the tree were her plates and cutlery, nicely washed and placed in a paper bag with a note that read, "If you seen us taking them, why didn't you say so?"[3]

The beach was important in Capi's life; she scavenged all of her wood for the fireplace. It was a bit wet and sandy, but it would do. Two friends once brought her a gift of Presto logs so that she would not have to burn wet wood and scraps from the beach. Capi thanked them but later said that it was one of the silliest gifts she had ever received; it was like bringing coals to Newcastle. On another occasion, as she and her daughter-in-law were driving into Victoria, they passed a house with a neatly stacked woodpile outside. Capi laughingly said, "They must come from the prairies." Janet's response was that it was the first time she had seen a good woodpile and Capi was not too thrilled with the comment. When so much wood littered the beaches, why would anyone spend money buying it, she wanted to know. However, driftwood is permeated with salt, which, when burned, produces an acid that over time, eats away at brick and causes chimney damage. Also, burning wood that has not been seasoned for six to nine months generates soot and creosote, which can markedly increase the risk of a chimney fire. Capi's friends' gift was wisely chosen, though she did not see it that way. After she died and her

Facing page: Capi and David's camp at Barkley Sound. COURTESY JANET BLANCHET

house was sold, it was not surprising that the new owners found the chimney seriously deteriorated.

While Capi's months-long forays along the coast ended with the sale of the *Caprice*, she did continue her travels, sometimes by sea and at other times by land. When David was discharged from the army in the early 1940s, he and his mother took a canoe trip on the west coast of Vancouver Island. They explored Barkley Sound and the Broken Islands Group, internationally known as a prime area for wilderness camping and kayaking. Although the Broken Group is protected from the large swells of the open ocean, Capi and David spent time paddling in open waters before they reached the inner sanctum of the hundred-plus islands. The area outside Barkley Sound is known as the "Graveyard of the Pacific," infamous for its numerous shipwrecks, fog, strong tidal currents and storm-force winds. Capi and David travelled in an open canoe, loaded with their tent and camping supplies. This could have been a recipe for disaster but Capi was not accident-prone; she always had a bit of sailor's luck on her side.

As Sidney and North Saanich grew, housing was difficult to obtain and land was at a premium. Capi's neighbours pointed out to her that her property was quite valuable and she should think about subdividing. After giving it much thought she did just that; the extra money would come in handy and allow her to do some travelling to warmer climates. She was not destitute by any means, but neither was she wealthy. She had some money invested in stocks and bonds, as well as a small estate trust from her grandfather and a pittance from her husband's bank pension. She was careful and had enough to live on, but nothing was left over for extravagances. She had a library of books worth thirty dollars. Her furniture was humble and well used, and her kitchen table was the butt of a number of jokes. It was definitely homespun—the top consisted of three substantial slabs of wood with gaps of five to seven centimetres between them, allowing for loose bits of anything to fall through—but it served its purpose well. Her dishes were chipped and mismatched. Her children used to laugh about Capi and her dishes. From time to time they would give her new mugs or glasses, replenishing her diminishing stock. They called it, "Giving Capi more glasses to break." She was not a Waterford Crystal kind of woman.

In 1952 she planned to spend the winter in the Caribbean. A friend of hers, a Mrs. Adams, had a winter home in St. Lucia and invited Capi to stay with her. The idea was that she would spend summers with Capi, and Capi would spend winters with her, but the plan did not work out; they were an unlikely pair. Mrs. Adams was very feminine, fond of pretty teacups and good china. She was always neatly attired in a dress or skirt, but she was also a bit strange. When she travelled she wore two or three dresses at the same time, one on top of the other. Capi had no interest in style; she was happy in her comfortable clothes and often walked to Sidney in her bib overalls and beat-up straw hat with a rucksack on her back. Mrs. Adams was chatty and lively while Capi was quiet and aloof. Capi had her own way of doing things and that was the way she liked it, so there was always tension between the two women.

Nevertheless, Mrs. Adams went on ahead to St. Lucia, expecting Capi to join her. Capi was to find her own way to New Orleans in time to take the weekly boat to the island, but her scheduling was off and she missed it. She found New Orleans daunting and instead of waiting around for a week she decided to take a bus to Puerto Vallarta in Mexico. She had rented her house out for the winter and couldn't go home; besides, the warmth would do her good. Although Sidney has its own microclimate, somewhat warmer and drier than Victoria, the winter months can be gloomy and wet.

Puerto Vallarta in the 1950s was a charming coastal village with cobblestoned streets, pink and orange bougainvillea draped over wrought-iron balconies and whitewashed buildings. It was a sleepy little town, off the beaten travel path. It did not become well known until 1963 when John Huston's filming of Tennessee Williams's play, *The Night of the Iguana*, at Mismaloya, a near-by fishing village, put Puerto Vallarta on the map. Capi could have gone by air, but as there were no direct flights from New Orleans, taking a bus sounded better to her, perhaps safer. The bus she boarded at the Mexican–US border was apparently a dishevelled wreck, the type of bus known to thrifty travellers as a "chicken bus." They are crammed to capacity with people, packages, farm goods and chickens. It was an unbearable trip for Capi. Crossing the Sierra Madre Mountains with their steep-sided canyons and rough terrain was terrifying, she said. The roads in the Sierra Madres are some of the most rugged and dangerous in the world. After riding more than 1,700 kilometres on the cramped bus, with its attendant odours, Capi changed her mind about flying. There was a jewel at the end of the trip, however, and she spent a lovely, lazy, warm winter walking the Malecón, the main seaside boardwalk, exploring the beaches and hiking in the jungles near Puerto Vallarta.

In the spring, Capi needed to take one more bus ride, a two hundred-kilometre trip due east to Guadalajara, before she could fly home. In Guadalajara she came down with a virus of some sort, and as she lay in her sick bed looking out at some large birds on the buildings nearby, her thoughts turned to vultures, those ominous-looking scavengers that prey on the wounded and the sick. She felt

that if she died in Guadalajara no one would ever know what had happened to her.

In 1957 Capi took another trip outside her home territory, flying to England to spend some time with her daughter, Elizabeth. While there she bought a Land Rover and travelled all over the United Kingdom, with forays into parts of Europe, including northwest France, enjoying the sights and scenes that were so different from coastal BC.

The post-war years were a busy time for Capi. In 1946 Little House was in a sad state and was torn down, its corner posts unable to support the house any longer. David set about designing and building his mother another house, higher up on the cliff, and by 1947 it was ready to move into, although the inside was never really completed. Capi insisted on doing some of the finishing work herself, and she worked on the interior bit by bit over the fourteen years she lived there. The house was an attractive, 111-square-metre bungalow of hollow tile construction with cedar panelling and fir flooring throughout. Some of the material used in the building was salvaged from Little House: the lovely, leaded, diamond-paned windows were used in the kitchen and bedrooms. The living room was spacious and had a vaulted ceiling, giving it a very airy appearance. However, there was no insulation in the ceiling and, as the single-paned windows offered little protection from the damp and cold, the temperature inside was often only slightly warmer than outside. Capi sometimes sat outside in her Adirondack chair, looking at Sidney Channel and appreciating the view.

Although central heating has been around since 2500 BC—even the ancient Romans had radiant, in-floor heat—Capi's only source of heat was a woodstove in the kitchen; the large fireplace in the living room sucked out what little warm air there was in the house. The stove needed constant attention because it would not stay alight for more than a half-hour at a time, and Janet Blanchet, who lived in the house with David and their baby daughter one winter, remembers that the nighttime temperatures would freeze the water in the kettle on the stove. She said, "Because Facing page: Puerto Vallarta. the bathroom remained a little warmer than the rest of the house we used to put our baby in her basket and place the basket on the bathroom sink pedestal overnight in order to take

advantage of the remaining heat from the fireplace vents. There was a curtain for the bathroom door, it was hung from a wooden rod that could readily be lifted from its pegs and moved to the door of the toilet room next door; those two rooms shared the curtain."[4]

Later, Capi traded the woodstove for an oil stove, but she was judicious about its use. In the summer months the stove, would not be lit until noon. To do otherwise, she felt, was imprudent and wasteful. That made cooking breakfast something of a challenge, but nothing that could not be overcome. Capi liked a poached egg for her morning meal so she developed an ingenious technique that bypassed the stove entirely. She would first heat water in the electric kettle. When it reached the boiling point she would pour it into in a pan, into which she broke the egg. She then placed the pan on an upturned iron that was held steady between two rocks. It worked perfectly, but a little patience was needed: the iron had to be set on "linen"—the highest setting—and it took seven to eight minutes.

Facing page, top: Capi in her Adirondack chair, beside the new house. Bottom: Northeast, ca. 1950.

COURTESY JANET BLANCHET

Over the years Capi developed emphysema, an irreversible, degenerative lung condition, perhaps due to living for years in damp, cold places. One of the treatments at the time was lung volume reduction surgery, but it had a high mortality rate so it was not really an option. Capi's doctor told her to move to a warmer, drier climate as cold weather could exacerbate her condition. Her response was to stick her head in the oven for twenty minutes a day; that was her dry climate, she said. Unfortunately, long-term exposure to oil stoves can cause the very condition she was trying to remedy.

Like its owner the new house had eccentricities. The entrance was actually through the kitchen because the front door never worked. The door itself was fine, but the handle had not been properly installed: when it was turned, it came off. There was also the issue of the pipes that carried water into the house. They were laid in a shallow trench, so if the ground was likely to freeze, the water had to be turned off to keep the pipes from bursting and anyone wanting water had to carry it in buckets from a well on the property. Janet remembers one winter having to rinse her baby's diapers in the ocean. It was so cold that even the saltwater along the shoreline was frozen. Capi had trouble with the well, too. There was iron in the water, which gave it an unpleasant taste, so she made a daily trek to her neighbours' to get water from their well instead. Over the years her well began to silt up, but digging a new well, or cleaning out the old one, would have been very expensive. Capi learned to make do.

In 1950 David began the construction of another house on the property, intended for Janet and himself, a little north of Capi's. Not surprisingly, they called it Northeast. The building was going along nicely when tragedy struck the family: in the autumn of 1953 David contracted poliomyelitis. He was hospitalized and recovered but remained paralyzed for the rest of his life. Naturally, all construction on the house stopped and it was put up for sale. Jack and Maxine Weber, a couple from Edmonton, bought the house in its unfinished state and brought in builders to complete it, planning to live there in the summers and spend the winters back in Alberta.

They knew little of their new neighbour, but their first meeting set them straight. Capi, in her usual blunt, straight-talking way, said, "You must understand that I am a person who does not like to see my neighbour's smoke."[5] Maxine said that she understood and was careful not to bother her. Years later, she related the incident to

Janet; at the time, she thought Capi was concerned that they would pester her with questions and ask her advice about the house. Capi continued to monitor the construction but quietly and from afar. Every day she walked to a bank above the building site and sat on her heels, watching the progress. She never announced her presence, but Maxine knew she was being observed. Capi and Maxine eventually became friends and often dropped in on each other. Maxine began to notice a pattern to these visits. Capi originally refused to have a television in her house but she liked the *I Love Lucy* show. It was from Maxine's well that Capi collected her water and Maxine said that Capi timed her trips to the well just as the program came on.

Capi also refused to have a telephone despite her children's pleas. She said the constant ringing of the phone would bother her; the neighbourhood shared a party line. The only way she was able to stay in contact with people was to write to them. She was very diligent about keeping in touch with her children. Elizabeth, Frances and Peter had moved away: Elizabeth lived in England, Frances in Golden, BC, and Peter at various times in Peru, Texas and Calgary.

In the fall of 1961, Capi and Maxine planned a trip to Tofino and Long Beach, before Maxine went back to Alberta for the winter, an adventure they were both looking forward to. There were no paved roads to Tofino, so the drive would be long and tedious and perhaps difficult. Capi was over at Northeast the evening before their departure, discussing the final arrangements, and, as they were to leave from there the next morning, Maxine suggested that Capi stay the night. Capi declined the offer. She said that she had a number of last-minute things to take care of; she had a loaf of bread to bake for the trip and she wanted to write to Peter.

The next morning, Maxine went over with the television set that

she was planning to lend Capi for the winter. The date was Friday, September 29; the morning was brisk but the daytime temperature was projected to rise to about 15°C. Maxine walked up the stone-flagged entry porch, opened the door and walked through into the kitchen. The table was in line with the door so it was the first thing she saw when entering through the small "mud room." Capi often took her typewriter into the kitchen to be near the warmth of the stove and that morning, the light was streaming through the adjacent windows, spotlighting the table and its lone occupant. Capi was slumped in her chair; an unfinished letter to Peter was in her typewriter and the bread that she was baking for the trip was still in the oven, burned beyond recognition. According to the coroner's report Capi had died of a cerebral haemorrhage sometime the previous evening. The interval between the onset of the stroke and death was thought to be approximately six hours.

Capi was just four months into her sixty-ninth year. Funeral services were held at the Sands Funeral Chapel of Roses in Sidney, on Tuesday, October 3. Her ashes were scattered on her beloved land at Curteis Point, where she had lived for thirty-eight years. A simple announcement appeared in the October 4 issue of the *Saanich Peninsula and Gulf Islands Review*: "Death Claims Local Author," was the headline. The article noted that Capi was a "Recognized writer of Canadiana and one of the pioneer residents of Curteis Point."[6]

Facing page: Part of Capi's property on Curteis Point, 2007.

CHAPTER SIX ✛

Capi's Children

It is hard to think of Elizabeth, Frances, Joan, Peter and David as growing up, getting older and eventually leaving their earthly experience behind. They have been pressed between the pages of *The Curve of Time* for the last forty-six years and have remained in a state of permanent stasis for its readers. But their lives did go on, and they did grow up; they married, bore children, had careers and suffered the infirmities and illnesses that go with life and old age. Capi raised strong, independent children who were exceptionally bright. They each put their stamp on the world and left an enduring legacy for their children and their children's children.

Their education was rich and varied. Having been home-schooled when she was young, Capi felt she could do a better job of educating her children than the public school system could. They took correspondence courses, and Capi had an engineer, who worked as a marine mechanic at the Canoe Cove marina, teach them their math, physics and chemistry. There was, of course, the backdrop of their summer travels to add practical experience to their curriculum. Capi did send David to a local public school for a time but she didn't think much of the quality of education he was getting, so she took him out. Peter went for a period to a private school in North

Facing page: Elizabeth, graduate of the Open University, 1991.
COURTESY JANET BLANCHET

Vancouver, but it was the two oldest girls, Elizabeth and Frances, who spent less time cruising up the coast and more in the school system. After their father's death they went to school for a year in Ottawa where they lived with their uncle and aunt, Guy and Eileen Blanchet. They were around thirteen and twelve at the time. After Ottawa they came back to Vancouver and spent two years with their Aunt Doris, Sister Liffiton, at the Convent of the Sacred Heart. Studies of home-schooling show that the children are usually as well socialized as those in the public school system, but Capi's lacked the ability to play with children their own age, to be silly, to let their hair down, and they were unacquainted with popular culture.[1] David, for one, thought those things were not worth knowing about. Whether it was an effect of the relative isolation they lived in or their responsibilities of being important members of the crew on the *Caprice*, they did not seem to fit the mould of, in this case, academic hypothesis.

After graduating from high school, Elizabeth and Frances both went on to study nursing. Elizabeth took her training at the Royal Jubilee Hospital in Victoria and graduated top in the province. She worked at the Vancouver General and the Montreal Children's hospitals and for a time in Bermuda, where she met and married her husband, who was stationed there with the British armed forces. After her daughter was born, she lived either with or near Capi and opened a daycare in Sidney. In 1946 she moved with her family to England, where she lived for the rest of her life. When her marriage ended she returned to nursing and continued her career until the mid-1950s. Then she took off her nurses' cap and became a very successful and well-known writer. She published over thirty novels, many of which can still be purchased.

Her writing career happened quite by chance: in 1955 *Good*

Housekeeping was producing a book on health titled *Pictorial Home Doctor, Your Guide to Good Health* and Elizabeth was asked to translate the medical jargon into popular parlance for the general public. She then incorporated her nursing experience into most of her books. While she wrote a few non-fiction books, most were novels of the romance genre with a nursing theme and her titles, such as *The Rebellion of Nurse Smith* or *Doctor Mark Temple*, were widely sought after. Elizabeth wrote under a variety of pseudonyms using Elizabeth Gilzean, Elizabeth Houghton and Mary Hunton. Houghton was her middle name and Hunton, which was Peter's middle name, was their paternal grandmother's maiden name. Her publisher, it seems, was not keen on having too many titles by the same author. Elizabeth was not certain what her mother thought of her writing, for Capi never said much.

While Elizabeth did not continue the adventurous outdoor lifestyle of her childhood, she did remain active. She enjoyed badminton and country dancing, she took art classes and swam fifty lengths a day, even after having heart surgery at eighty-one. In 1991, at the age of seventy-eight, she earned an honours degree in social sciences and world politics at Open University. She died on October 12, 1995; she was eighty-two.

Frances studied nursing at the Vancouver General Hospital. After she graduated she worked for two years in a hospital in Golden, British Columbia, where she met her husband-to-be, Ron King. He once teasingly said that when they first met he thought she was bossy. She had been, after all, one of the senior nurses at the hospital. Golden, which is near the Alberta border, is a vibrant Rocky Mountain community nestled in the Columbia River Valley. Frances and Ron were married in 1946 and had a June wedding—"pretty," according to the newspaper. The description read, "The bride, looking very sweet, wore a navy silk bolero effect frock trimmed with white eyelet embroidery . . . flowers were sweetheart rapture roses en corsage . . . Following the impressive ceremony a buffet breakfast was held at the groom's home where relatives and immediate friends gathered around a beautifully arranged table gaily flowered with peonies."[2] Frances's father-in-law, Thomas King, was the member of the legislative assembly for the area and had a ranch just outside Golden. Frances and her husband ran a ranch on which they raised Hereford cattle. They had three children; a son who died tragically at a young age, a daughter and an adopted son. They were able to celebrate their fiftieth wedding anniversary just before Frances died in 1996, at eighty-two.

Joan, Capi's third child, became an artist and, later in life, an accomplished gardener. Always drawing, she honed her talent at the Vancouver Art School (now the Emily Carr Institute of Art + Design) and then at the Art Students League in New York, a prestigious school where many of the top American artists have either studied or taught. To test her resolve, and to see if she was up for New York, Joan bought an old canoe for five dollars and paddled it from Vancouver to Curteis Point. She felt if she could do that, she could confront New York. It took her five days, with one night of non-stop paddling for nine hours, to get to Vancouver Island. She crossed the Strait of Georgia at night because she said that the weather was usually calmer at night and she wanted to avoid the daytime marine-related traffic. It was perhaps a bit foolish, for large, deep-sea ships would not have been able to see anything as small as a canoe out on the open waters at night. When she finally pulled up in front of her mother's house, exhausted from her ordeal and quite proud of herself, she expected praise. Instead,

Capi seemed angry and said, "Just because I'm a fool doesn't mean you children have to be!"[3] However, she apparently laughed herself to sleep that night. Joan married and had one daughter. Like her mother, she enjoyed her solitude. Joan died on May 15, 1999, just one day into her eighty-third year.

Peter, quite a brilliant young man, entered the University of British Columbia when he was only sixteen, becoming a mining engineer and geologist. He did innovative work in the use of aerial surveying and photography for the purpose of oil exploration and worked on a type of memory rod before the advent of computers— IBM wanted to work with Peter on it as early as the late 1940s. He and his wife spent some time in Peru and then Houston, Texas, working for one of the oil companies. Later they moved to Calgary. Peter eventually left the oil company and pursued his own business ventures. In time he moved back to BC, started up International Geosystems Corporation, or Golden Tech, and introduced Gelog software to the mining industry; it analyzed assays and provided important feedback about the ingredients and quality of metals and ores. Peter loved the game of chess and taught his son, Richard, to play at the age of five. Richard said that it was many years before he could finally beat his father properly. Peter and his wife raised thirteen children; they had nine of their own and adopted four. Peter was seventy-eight when he died in 1997.

David was equally brilliant. He had an IQ of 182 on the Stanford-Binet Intelligence Scale; a score of 132 and above is a "very superior" rating. He entered UBC when he was seventeen, confident in his intellectual abilities and not affected by the goal to be first in his class. Such rankings were of no interest to him; it was knowledge and information that piqued his curiosity. He had spent a year studying at UBC when he decided to join the army. Because of his abilities, he was commissioned as an instructor at an officers' training camp. Ironically, he was not allowed to take the training himself, as he was considered too young to go overseas as a soldier. Thinking he would never have the chance to get to the main theatres of operation in Europe, he transferred to the air force and became a navigator. However, he became ill with measles, which turned into bilateral pneumonia and pleurisy. This left him in a weakened state and he had no option but to leave the armed forces.

He went back to UBC but could not settle on a program of studies, so he quit and began designing and building houses. He married Janet Patterson, who lived near David and his mother; she was the daughter of R. M. Patterson, a celebrated Canadian author who wrote about his trips into the Canadian wilderness and life on an Alberta ranch. Janet and David had a daughter and when their house, Northeast, had a roof on and walls put up, the family moved in. It was chilly and draughty, as the doors had not yet been hung, and they spent most of their time in the kitchen—the warmest place in the house. But even in its unfinished state, Janet said, it offered more protection than their previous residence: they had spent two summers living in a tent while David worked on the house. Their little girl was just four years old when her father contracted polio in 1953.

They had all attended a Halloween party given by a neighbour. There was a polio epidemic sweeping across the country, but most people did not give it much thought. It was a disease that mainly affected children. After the party, several people began experiencing the telltale stiff neck, headaches, fever and muscle pain that signalled the onset of polio. Four or five children came down with the disease; David was the only adult. He was twenty-nine at the time. Polio is a devastating virus that affects the central nervous system and can result in muscle paralysis, weakness, serious physical deformities, lifelong disability or death. For adults the virus was even more virulent than for children; many died, spent years in an iron lung or were partially paralyzed, their lives forever altered. David was in the hospital and in rehabilitation for two years. He came out with his life but was confined to a wheelchair for the rest of it. He was given only two years but he managed to live until he was fifty-seven. His breathing was so laboured from a weakened diaphragm, resulting from the polio, that it put a strain on his heart, and in the end he died of heart failure.

✤ ✤ ✤

Maxine Weber lived at Northeast for another thirty-one years until her suspicious death on April 13, 1992. She and her partner, Bob Swanson, were planning to go to Alberta that day. The evening before, they had been in the hot tub, as was their usual practice. Arlene, the woman who was going to house-sit for them, came to pick them up in the morning to take them to the airport, expecting to find suitcases by the door and two people ready. Instead she found them still in the hot tub, dead. They were careful, responsible people, in good health. Maxine was found face down in the tub and Bob was seated. There was no explanation and the cause of death, if known, has never been made public. There have been suggestions that an unscrupulous real estate agent was keen to get his hands on the property rather too soon after they died. Their deaths remain a mystery, but some people think it was the result of foul play.

EPILOGUE ✛

Muriel Wylie Blanchet was many things to many people. She has been described as intelligent, unusual, an odd sort of person, abrasive, difficult and arrogant. She was not a vain woman, and yet she was not immune to the attention she received when she donned her summer sailing uniform—a smart-looking pair of shorts. She also enjoyed the nods over the "*très chic*" clam-diggers she wore while travelling in France with her daughter Elizabeth. That she was strong is without question; she prided herself on her vigour. Capi never felt that age should make a difference to anyone's activities. Whenever her grandchildren asked her age she always retorted, "I'm one hundred." She was resilient and adventurous; some called her foolhardy. At times she tempted fate and pushed her knowledge and strength to the edge by taking her boat and children into conditions that could be considered dangerous. She was a composed sort of person, not easily ruffled and never apologetic. Her publisher, Gray Campbell, described Capi as "matter-of-fact friendly, unassuming, with a no-nonsense side trying to hide a shy but rich sense of humour."[1] She was guarded with strangers, certainly not a joyous or spontaneous type of person, but she loved children and was very good to them, although some of her grandchildren were terrified of her. She lacked social graces and preferred solitude to spending time with neighbours or her community, and as she grew older she cherished her privacy even more. Her property, for example, had no sign with her name. "If people did not know where she lived (that is, if she had not informed them) she was not interested in seeing them."[2]

But Capi was more than her public persona. The writing in *The Curve of Time* and *A Whale Named Henry* shows a sensitive person, someone who is attuned to subtle nuances and dimensions of colour unseen by others. One friend said that she was repressed. She was a mystery, another said. It was suggested that even her own sons did not really know their mother.

It is hard to shoehorn someone like Capi into one paradigm of character traits. Each person presents many selves to the world, unconsciously matching the particular circumstance at hand. In many cases she was not much different from the characters she met along the coast, those who had to rely on their strength of character and self-sufficiency to survive. Her life was full and challenging; she did not need the company of strangers nor did she welcome superficial conversation. Her growing reclusiveness was probably influenced in part by the type of life she had led: she had to care for her children, who took up most of her time for quite a number of years, and later she helped care for David and Janet's daughter after David became ill. And she lived apart. Her home on Curteis Point was out of the way and quite secluded, and all the years she had spent sailing along the coast added to her independence. Reclusiveness can be a recurring personality trait and in Capi's case it may have been—one daughter and a granddaughter were similar. Her friends understood this part of her nature and were extremely loyal to and fiercely protective of her.

Capi Blanchet remains an enigma, for she left only the books she wrote and the photographs she took as material from which her life story could be scripted. That she was a superb storyteller is without question; she artfully drew her readers into an enchanting world from which they don't want to emerge. But behind the books was a remarkable woman: one who set her own standards, in a financially precarious and more masculine time. She never shied away from life's difficulties—to her they were snags or hitches—but she dealt with some more skilfully than others. Her life was at times wonderful and at times hard, but the uniting strands were her resilience, her integrity, her honesty and her determination. She was the leading lady, the female protagonist of her story; she was who she was, for which lovers of the British Columbia coast can be grateful.

ENDNOTES ✢

Introduction: Capi Blanchet and *The Curve of Time*

[1] Capi's story about Henry the whale was rediscovered when Edith Iglauer was doing research on her for an article she was writing for the *Raincoast Chronicles* no. 8 in 1983. It was published posthumously, first as "Henry Finds the Roar," *Raincoast Chronicles Six/Ten* (Madeira Park: Harbour Publishing, 1983) 157–164; and then as *A Whale Named Henry* (Madeira Park: Harbour Publishing 1983).

[2] M. Wylie Blanchet, *The Curve of Time*, 10th ed. (North Vancouver: Whitecap Books, 2004), Foreword.

[3] The names of the children can be a bit confusing. In *The Curve of Time* Joan is Jan and David is John, which was his first name. Peter was referred to in the family as Tate and Elizabeth as Betty. For consistency I will use the children's birth names throughout the book.

[4] Gary Powell, Customer rating on Amazon.com, December 31, 2003.

[5] Michele Belanger-Mcnair, Customer rating on Amazon.com, November 28, 2000.

[6] The magazine was named *Atlantic Monthly* from 1857–1932, changed to *The Atlantic* from 1932–1971, and is currently called *Atlantic Monthly*. I was unable to find any of her publications in the magazine, even after looking though the archives of the *Atlantic Monthly*.

[7] Gray Campbell, preface to *The Curve of Time*, n.p.

[8] Cornish's was the only bookstore and lending library in Sidney in 1961. It is likely that this is the store to which Capi provided the loan.

[9] There are many spellings for coastal First Nations tribes and villages. I have followed the spellings throughout this book using the U'mista Cultural Centre's orthography as developed by Jay Powell and Gloria Cranmer Webster in the 1970s.

[10] Capi refers to Bullock Bluff as Bullock Point.

[11] Distance on marine charts is represented in nautical miles. A nautical mile is an international system of units in which one nautical mile is equal to 1.852 kilometres or 0.998383 geographical miles.

Chapter One: Capi's Early Life

[1] Letter to Alan Mathias Snetsinger in Little Métis from John Gray Goodall Snetsinger, July 13 1895.

[2] "Insolvent Notice: C.A. Liffiton and The Acme Spice and Coffee Mills," *Globe and Mail* (Monday, October 22, 1900): 22.

[3] Letter to Miss Violet Nicholas Liffiton, Quebec, from Charles A. Liffiton, 133 Metcalf St., Montreal, sent Sunday evening, undated. Courtesy of Tom Liffiton, 2006.

[4] M. Wylie Blanchet, *The Curve of Time*, 10th ed. (North Vancouver: Whitecap Books, 2004) 124–125.

[5] Letter to Mrs. C.A. Liffiton c/o C.A. Liffiton Esq. Commercial Union Bldg. St. James St., Montreal, Quebec via New York Str. RMS. *Lusitania*, May 20, 191? Courtesy of Tom Liffiton, 2006.

[6] Blanchet, 42.

[7] Blanchet, 152.

[8] "Doris Liffiton RSCH 1896-1957," Translated from the French transcript of the *Annual Letters of the Society of Sacred Heart of Jesus* (1957–1958–1959), vol. 1, 3rd section. Courtesy Tom Liffiton.

[9] Janet Blanchet, e-mail, June 2, 2006.

[10] Records indicate that Doris Liffiton studied at the University of Rome. At the time there was only one such university, which was founded in 1303.

[11] Janet Blanchet, e-mail, 2006.

[12] Blanchet, 151.

[13] Lynda Dionne and George Pelletier, et al. *Essaies sur l'histoire Civile et Sociale de Cacouna*, (Cacouna, QC: 1975). Translated by Viateur Beaulieu. http://cacouna.net

[14] A text description of the Snetsinger Villa's history is on a plaque in front of the house. "The site of the house, on the south side of the road, is . . . unique, as the other villas and summer cottages stand on the north side of the road, along the cliff overlooking the water. The house originally stood on the church road. It was built in 1854 by Pierre Gosselin, a local carpenter. He had been hired by the architect and sculptor Francois-Xavier Berlinguette . . . Five years later, Monsieur Berlinguette ceded the house to Pierre Gosselin as a balance of payment. In 1861, a young, recently married farmer named Félix F. Gagnon bought the house and had it moved to its present location on this piece. He rented it to tourists for several years before selling it in 1876 to John Gray Goodall Snetsinger." Lynda Dionne and Georges Pelletier, "Cacouna les randonnées du passé." Viateur Beaulieu, e-mail, December, 5, 2006.

[15] M. Gagnon. *Regional Assessment: St. Lawrence Lower Estuary Priority Intervention Zone 18*, (Ottawa, ON: Environment Canada Quebec Region, 1997).

[16] The Dominion of Canada created the Post Office Department in 1867.

[17] Letter to David and Janet Blanchet from Elizabeth, at Compton, Berkshire, England, June 8, 1976. Courtesy of Janet Blanchet.

[18] Edith Iglauer, "'Capi' Blanchet," *The Strangers Next Door* (Madeira Park: Harbour Publishing, 1991), 225.

[19] Letter to David from Elizabeth, June 8, 1976.

[20] Willys-Overland Ltd., advertisement, Toronto, Ontario, 1923.

[21] Iglauer, 225.

[22] Editorial, *Sidney and Islands Review*, December 4, 1924.

[23] Blanchet, 159.

[24] The Latch received its name in the 1940s reportedly as a result of the fact that all doors in the house had a latch. Today The Latch is a charming inn and restaurant that showcases much of the interior as it was originally built in 1926. It is said that a gentle ghost frequents it from time to time. For information on The Latch, see www. latchinn.ca

[25] Letter to Janet Blanchet from Martin Segger at the British Columbia Provincial Museum, April 11, 1975. Courtesy of Janet Blanchet.

[26] Letter to Martin Segger from Janet Blanchet, North Vancouver, BC, April 11, 1975. Courtesy of Janet Blanchet.

[27] Mr. Moresby-White married Miss Leigh Pemberton, daughter of Sir Edward Leigh Pemberton and Lady Leigh Pemberton in London, England, on November 3, 1914. *The British Colonist* (Vancouver Island, BC), November 28, 1914.

[28] In addition to Moresby-White's property, about forty hectares of adjacent land was owned a Mr. Carew with whom Moresby-White was associated. The two properties together were to be part of a land development. Letter written to Martin Segger by Janet Blanchet, April 30, 1975. Courtesy of Janet Blanchet.

[29] Letter to David from Elizabeth, June 8, 1976.

[30] A magneto is an electrical generator that supplies electricity to the spark plugs. It provides a high-voltage pulse rather than a continuous current. It creates less drag than does the battery-coil systems. Also, as there are no wires connecting components there is greater operational reliability. The Kermath Manufacturing Company stopped manufacturing engines sometime in 1956 or 1957.

[31] Letter to David from Elizabeth, June 8, 1976.

[32] Letter to David from Elizabeth, June 8, 1976.

[33] Letter to David from Elizabeth, June 8, 1976.

[34] Letter to David from Elizabeth, June 8, 1976.

[35] *The Daily Colonist*, September 11, 1926.

[36] Letter to David from Elizabeth, June 8, 1976.

[37] Letter to David from Elizabeth, June 8, 1976.

[38] Blanchet, 161–162.

[39] Blanchet, 162.

[40] Blanchet, 162.

[41] Janet Blanchet, "Recollections of Capi Blanchet." Personal papers.

Chapter Two: After Geoffrey's Death—Preparing for Cruising

1 Janet Blanchet, "Recollections of Capi Blanchet." Personal papers.

2 Janet Blanchet, e-mail, June 26, 2006.

3 Edith Iglauer, "Capi Blanchet," *The Strangers Next Door* (Medeira Park: Harbour Publishing, 1991), 228.

4 Letter to David from Elizabeth, June 8, 1976.

5 Iglauer, 226.

6 Blanchet, 156.

7 Blanchet, 3.

8 Blanchet, 4.

9 Blanchet, 24.

10 Blanchet, 18.

11 Blanchet, 76.

12 Blanchet, 57.

13 Blanchet, 58.

14 Blanchet, 60.

15 *Sailing Directions: British Columbia Coast (South Portion)*, (Minister of Fisheries and Oceans Canada), vol.1, 16th ed., 359.

16 Blanchet, 63.

17 Blanchet, 64.

Chapter Three: Cruising Princess Louisa Inlet and Desolation Sound

1 M. Wylie Blanchet, *The Curve of Time*, 10th ed. (North Vancouver: Whitecap Books, 2004), 5.

2 Blanchet, 8.

3 Princess Louisa Inlet was originally known by the Sechelt people as Swíwelát. This name referred to a village site at the mouth of the inlet but additionally meant "sunny and warm." The water temperature is a comfortable 20° C in July and August.

[4] Blanchet, 11.

[5] Blanchet, 14.

[6] I have followed the spelling of Macdonald used by The Princess Louisa Society and Bruce Calhoun, the author of *Mac and the Princess: The Story of Princess Louisa Inlet and James Macdonald.* BC Parks Department uses the spelling MacDonald.

[7] Thomas Foster Hamilton, 1894–1969, was a pioneer and innovator in aviation and was president of United Airports. He revolutionized propulsion technology of propeller-driven aircraft and started the Malibu SeaAero Airlines to service his resort.

[8] Blanchet, 16.

[9] Chuck Gould, "Trappers Cabin," *Waggoner Cruising Guide: The Complete Boating Reference* (Bellevue, WA: Robert Hale and Co., Weatherly Press Division, 2006), 200.

[10] Blanchet, 15.

[11] The *Caprice* probably averaged around 5 knots.

[12] Blanchet, 35.

[13] Robin Fisher, *Vancouver's Voyage: Charting the Northwest Coast 1791–1795*, 226.

[14] Hugh Ackroyd, Sunshine Coast Area Supervisor, BC Parks, e-mail, Sept. 7. 2006.

[15] Melanie Cove and Laura Cove are two of the many protected anchorages in Prideaux Haven. Prideaux Haven is located at Latitude 50°09'N., Longitude 124°41'W. It is at the entrance to Homfray Channel and is part of Desolation Sound Marine Park.

[16] Blanchet, 43.

[17] Blanchet, 43.

Chapter Four: Cruising Beyond Desolation Sound

[1] M. Wylie Blanchet, *The Curve of Time*, 10th ed. (North Vancouver: Whitecap Books, 2004), 115.

[2] Province of British Columbia, 1966. Highway sign.

[3] Blanchet, 114.

[4] Blanchet, 114.

[5] Blanchet, 114.

[6] Frances Duncan, *The Sayward-Kelsey Bay Saga*, 50.

[7] The term Kwakwaka'wakw is a term used by the U'mista Cultural Centre and loosely means "Kwak'wala speaking people." There is no historical precedence for this name as there is not a strong sense of a Kwakwaka'wakw national identity. In the past people identified with their communities, their villages and their tribes. It is a term that is becoming more accepted. The term used by Boas in 1897 was Kwakiutl, which was an inaccurate transcription. The phonetic interpretation is kʷaguł, or kʷaguʔł.

[8] Blanchet, 44.

[9] Treaties were not signed in British Columbia betweem 1899 and 1973, but the government-designated certain lands as reserves. Groups or tribes that sometimes lived together were broken up, assigned the term "band" and allocated a particular government designated village. The "bands" changed the form of governing from hereditary chiefs to chiefs and councils that are elected by the members of the community.

[10] Blanchet, 73.

[11] Blanchet, 45.

[12] Blanchet, 66.

[13] In the 1700s there were an estimated 19,000 people, but by the 1920s the number had dwindled to fewer than two thousand people. "Adapting to Uncertain Futures: Alert Bay Community Background Report," draft, Sept. 2006, 26.

[14] Permission from the appropriate band offices would be appreciated before landing on the village sites. Also, provincial regulations prohibit disturbing archaeological sites and objects.

[15] The name Tsadzis'nukwaame' means "eel grass out in front." The

people also called the village New Vancouver because it is north facing like the beach in Vancouver. Jay Stewart and Peter Macnair, *To the Totem Forests*, an exhibition catalogue (1999).

16 *Sailing Directions: British Columbia Coast (South Portion)*, 340.

17 *Waggoner Cruising Guide: The Complete Boating Reference 2006*, 251.

18 Blanchet, 172.

19 Qalogwis has several different writings. According the Museum at Campbell River, Ḵalugwis and Karlukwees are two common spellings. The U'mista orthography uses Ḵalugwis.

20 The reserve allowed a per capita allocation of 0.942 hectares. The commissioners from the McKenna-McBride Royal Commission on Indian Affairs felt that the amount of land was inadequate for maintaining a sustainable life. The Ławitsis put forth further claims to increase their territory. They were given four other reserves nearby, but it did not add significantly to their territory.

21 Jay Stewart and Peter Macnair, *To the Totem Forests*, an exhibition catalogue, 1999, 24.

22 Capi refers to Native Anchorage as Indian Anchorage.

23 Chief Dan Cranmer's wife's relatives were from 'Mi'mkwamlis.

24 James P. Spradley, ed., *Guests Never Leave Hungry: The Autobiography of James Sewid, a Kwakiutl Indian* (New Haven, MA: Yale University Press, 1960), 122–31.

25 Emily Carr used dsnokoa (Dxo'noq!wa), which was taken from the lexicon established by Boas. Boas also uses the spelling Ts'o'noqoa. The U'mista orthography uses dzunuḵwa.

26 The Carr Papers 1905-1946, BC Archives MS-2181 Reel A1227, Box 7, Fol 33 & 34, Carr Lecture of Totems, 1913:49–50; Jay Stewart and Peter Macnair, *To The Totem Forests*, 1999.

27 Blanchet, 47.

28 Blanchet, 49.

29 The original painting on the house front was a sea monster, but when

Chief Johnny Scow remarried he rebuilt the house. The house front was repainted with a raven, which was part of his wife's dowry. Peter Macnair, personal communication with the author, May 16, 2007.

[30] Beth Hill, *Upcoast Summers*, 123.

[31] Howard White and Jim Spilsbury, *Spilsbury's Coast*, 157. Jim Spilsbury was a best-selling author who chronicled life along the coast of BC from the 1930s to the 1960s. He built vital communications networks along the coast, provided coastal air transport and founded Queen Charlotte Airlines. He received the Order of BC in 1993, the highest award given by the province to honour those who have served their lives with distinction, benefitting citizens in the province or elsewhere.

[32] Blanchet, 53. During times of potlatch, copper bracelets were sometimes scattered on the mudflats. It could have been one of these that Capi found.

[33] Hill, 123.

[34] Bill Proctor and Yvonne Maximchuk, *Full Moon, Flood Tide*, 113.

[35] Ba'a's is sometimes spelled Pahas or Paás.

[36] The 'Nak̓waxda'x̱w had summer hunting, fishing and trapping stations throughout Seymour Inlet, Frederick Sound, Belize Inlet, Alison Sound and Shelter Bay.

[37] Willie Seaweed was born in 1873 in Nugent Sound and became Chief Hilamas of the 'Nak̓waxda'x̱w. He was a master carver whose work has been exhibited throughout the world. His influence can be seen in the works of many young carvers today.

[38] Blanchet, 68.

[39] Edward S. Curtis, "The Kwakiutl," *The North American Indian*, Vol. 10, 1915, 307.

[40] Edward Curtis was a pioneer cinematographer of the early twentieth century who documented the many First Nations groups of North America. The film was a story of love and revenge, and Curtis paid meticulous attention to detail of the canoes, dancing, rituals and

clothing of pre-contact times. The film was initially titled *In the Land of the Headhunters*.

41 The Gws'Sala and 'Nak'waxda'xw (British Columbia, *Report of the Royal Commission on Aboriginal Peoples*, volume 1: 1996,), 3.

42 Blanchet, 81.

43 Blanchet, 81.

44 Blanchet, 84.

45 The *Blue Fjord* was the *PML 15* (police motor launch) but was originally built in 1931 for the minister of public works as *Milwin*. It was last operated as a charter vessel, working for thirty years along the BC coast. It sank in Tribune Channel, which circles Gilford Island and feeds into Knight Inlet.

46 Mike Durban in conversation with Jean Compton of *The Chronicle*, December 12, 2005.

47 Blanchet, 82.

48 Proctor and Maximchuk, 188.

49 Tim McGrady, Operations Manager of Knight Inlet Lodge, e-mail, May 16, 2007.

50 Knight Inlet Lodge, "Environmental Stewardship." http://www. knightinlet.com/stewardship.html

51 Blanchet, 85.

52 Blanchet, 85.

53 Ian and Karen McAllister, *Canada's Great Bear Rainforest*, vol. 18, no. 1, 1999, Special Edition, co-published with the Raincoast Conservation Society. http://www.wildernesscommittee.org/ campaigns/historic/memberreport/reports/Vol19No01/greatbear

54 The Nature Conservancy of Canada. Press release from ForestEthics, Greenpeace, Sierra Club, Jan. 21, 2007.

55 The Da'naxda'xw were closely related to the A'wa'etlala, who also lived in Knight Inlet. Around 1860 they amalgamated, and in 1890 they found their way to T'sadzis'nukwaame (New Vancouver) on

Harbledown Island, where many have recently relocated. Their traditional territory is in the mountainous region at the head of Knight Inlet up to around Kleena Kleene, as well as the watershed area of the Klinaklini River.

56 "Preserving the Tradition of T'lina Making," Community Memories, U'Mista Cultural Centre. www.virtualmuseum.ca

Chapter Five: Life after the *Caprice*

1 Capi was reported to have made a trip around Vancouver Island with a friend, but that was in the *Caprice*, not the *Scylla*. Personal conversation with Janet Blanchet.

2 Janet Blanchet, "Recollections of Capi Blanchet." Personal papers.

3 Janet Blanchet, "Recollections of Capi Blanchet." Personal papers.

4 Janet Blanchet, "Recollections of Capi Blanchet." Personal papers.

5 Janet Blanchet, "Recollections of Capi Blanchet." Personal papers.

6 *Saanich Peninsula and Gulf Islands Review*, October 4, 1961.

Chapter Six: Capi's Children

1 Janet Blanchet, e-mail, August 29, 2006.

2 Newspaper article, unknown source, Golden, BC, 1941. In "Notes on the Family of John Gray Goodall Snetsinger and His Wife Margaret Irving," prepared by Rosemary Joy, 1986.

3 Janet Iglauer, "Capi Blanchet," *The Strangers Next Door* (Medeira Park: Harbour Publishing, 1991), 227.

Epilogue

1 Gray Campbell, preface to *The Curve of Time*, n.p.

2 Janet Blanchet, "Recollections of Capi Blanchet." Personal papers.

SELECTED BIBLIOGRAPHY ✢

Books and Articles

Bingham, Janet. *Samuel Maclure, Architect.* Ganges, BC: Horsdal & Schubart, 1985.

Blanchet, Janet. "Recollections of Capi Blanchet." Unpublished.

Blanchet, M. Wylie. *The Curve of Time.* North Vancouver, BC: Whitecap Books, 10th edition, 1990. First published 1961 by William Blackwood & Sons Ltd., London. First Canadian Edition 1968 by Gray's Publishing.

———. "Henry Finds the Roar." In *Raincoast Chronicles Six/Ten: Collector's Edition*, edited by Howard White, 157–64. Madeira Park, BC: Harbour Publishing, 1983.

———. *A Whale Named Henry.* Madeira Park, BC: Harbour Publishing, 1983.

British Admiralty Charts 1848–1955. Series CM/ES1. BC Archives and Record Services.

British Admiralty Charts in the Historical Map Collection. Special Collections UBC Library, G3511 .P5 svar G7.

British Colonist. "Moresby-White Married Leigh Pemberton." November 13, 1914.

British Columbia. *First Peoples Heritage, Language and Culture Act*, RSBC 1996, c.147. Victoria, BC: Queen's Printer.

British Columbia. *Heritage Conservation Act*, RSBC 1996, c. 187. Victoria, BC: Queen's Printer.

British Columbia. "Ministry of Aboriginal Relations and Reconciliation 2007/08-2009/10 Service Plan." Victoria, BC: Ministry of Aboriginal Relations and Reconciliation.

British Columbia. *Royal Commission on Indian Affairs for the Province of British Columbia 1913-1916.* McKenna and McBride, co-chairs. Victoria, BC: Acme Press, 1916.

British Columbia. Vital Statistics. Vital Event Death Registration: Muriel
Wylie Blanchet. Reg. no. 1961-09-011165, Microfilm no. B13253.
BC Archives and Records Services.

British Columbia Provincial Archives and Provincial Museum. *Our
Native Peoples.* Victoria, BC: Provincial Archives, 1952–66.

British Columbia Supreme Court Probate. Estate of Geoffrey Orme
Blanchet. December 14, 1926. GR 1553, vol. 14, Letters of
Administration January 1926–May 1929. BC Archives and Records
Services.

————. Estate Files 1859–1941. GR 1304, 304/1926, Box 290, File 2.
BC Archives and Records Services.

Canada. Royal Commission on Aboriginal Peoples. René Dussault
and Georges Erasmus, co-chairs. *Report of the Royal Commission on
Aboriginal Peoples.* Ottawa, ON: Canadian Communication Group,
1996.

Canadian Hydrographic Service. *Canadian Tide and Current Tables.* Vols.
5, 6, 7. Ottawa, ON: Fisheries and Oceans Canada, 2007.

Carr, Emily. "Lecture on Totems," 1913. MSS 1227, Box 7, Fol. 33, 34.
BC Archives and Records Service.

Chamberlin, David R. "Architectural Plans of Samuel Maclure and Other
Architects." UVIC Special Collections. Architect: Samuel Maclure,
Client: A. Moresby White, 1915. File Drawing Nos. AP1243-
AP1246, AP2022-AP2026, Location Index File #127.

Curtis, Edward S. *The Kwakiutl.* Vol. 10 in *The North American Indian:
The Indians of the United States, the Dominion of Canada, and Alaska.*
Norwood, MA: The Plimpton Press, 1915.

Daily Colonist. "Boat Abandoned: Drowning Feared. Godfrey [Geoffrey]
O. Blanchet Missing From Launch Found Off Knapp Island."
September 11, 1926. BC Archives Microfilms, *Victoria Daily
Colonist* 1926, Box 1926.

Day, Beth. *Grizzlies in their Backyard.* Surrey, BC: Heritage House, 1994.

Director General Canadian Hydrographic Service. *Sailing Directions:*

British Columbia Coast, South Portion., vol. 1, ed. 16. Ottawa, ON: Fisheries and Oceans Canada, 1999.

Duff, Wilson. *The Indian History of British Columbia: Impact of the White Man*. 3rd ed. Victoria, BC: Royal British Columbia Museum, 1997.

Duncan, Frances. *The Sayward-Kelsey Bay Saga (Eighty-Eight Years at Sayward-Kelsey Bay)*. Courtenay, BC: Argus Publishing Co., 1958.

"Doris Liffiton RSCJ 1869-1957." *Annual Letters of the Society of the Sacred Heart of Jesus*. Vol. 1, 1957–1958–1959.

Fisher, Robin. *Vancouver's Voyage: Charting the Northwest Coast, 1791-1795*. Vancouver, BC: Douglas & McIntyre, 1992.

Francis, Daniel. *A Road for Canada: The Illustrated Story of the Trans-Canada Highway*. North Vancouver, BC: Stanton Atkins and Dosil Publishers, 2006.

Fry, Alan. *How a People Die*. Madeira Park, BC: Harbour Publishing, 1994. First published 1970 by Doubleday & Company.

Gagnon, M. *Regional Assessment: St. Lawrence Lower Estuary Priority Intervention Zone 18*. Ottawa, ON: Environment Canada Quebec Region, 1997.

Galois, Robert. *Kwakwaka'wakw Settlement, 1775–1920: A Geographical Analysis and Gazetteer*. Vancouver, BC: University of British Columbia Press, 1994.

Gardner, Robert with William Heick. "Blunden Harbour." Watertown, MA: Documentary Educational Resources, 1951. DVD.

———. "Dances of the Kwakiutl." Seattle, WA: Orbit Films, 1951. Filmstrip. Watertown, MA: Documentary Educational Resources. DVD.

Grant, Peter. *The Story of Sidney*. Victoria, BC: Porthole Press, 1998.

Greenpeace, Forest Ethics, Sierra Club of Canada, BC Chapter. *The Roadmap to Change: A 2006 Progress Report on the Great Bear Rainforest Agreements*. Document. December 20, 2006.

Grundmann, Erika. *Dark Sun: Te Rapunga and the Quest of George Dibben*. Auckland, NZ: David Ling Publishing, 2004.

Harold, Hughina. *Totem Poles and Tea.* Surrey, BC: Heritage House, 1996.

Hill, Beth. *Upcoast Summers.* Ganges, BC: Horsdal & Schubart, 1985.

Homfeld, Max F. "Who Was James Kermath, and the Kermath Manufacturing Company?" *Gas Engine Magazine.* Topeka, KS: Ogden Publications. http://www.gasenginemagazine.com/complete-archive/3563

Isenor, Dick and E. G. Stephens and D. E. Watson. *Edge of Discovery: A History of the Campbell River District.* Campbell River, BC: Ptarmigan Press, 1989.

Iglauer, Edith. *The Strangers Next Door.* Madeira Park, BC: Harbour Publishing, 1991.

Jonaitis, Aldona, ed. *Chiefly Feasts: The Enduring Kwakiutl Potlatch.* New York: American Museum of Natural History, 1991.

Joy, Rosemary A. "The Genealogy of John Gray Goodall Snetsinger 1833–1909." Revised 1996. Kingston, ON.

Kennedy, Liv. *Coastal Villages.* Madeira Park, BC: Harbour Publishing, 1991.

Kirk, Ruth. *Widsom of the Elders: Native Tradition on the Northwest Coast, the Nuu-chah-nulth, Southern Kwakiutl and Nuxalk.* Vancouver, BC: Douglas & McIntyre, 1988.

Lange, Owen, ed. *Marine Weather Hazards Manual: A Guide to Local Forecasts and Conditions.* 2nd ed. Ottawa, ON: Environment Canada, 1990.

McAllister, Ian and Karen McAllister with Cameron Young. *The Great Bear Rainforest: Canada's Forgotten Coast.* Madeira Park, BC: Harbour Publishing, 1997.

Menzies, Archibald. *Menzies' Journal of Vancouver's Voyage: April to October 1792.* Victoria, BC: Legislative Assembly of British Columbia, 1923; Archibald Menzies fonds: 1754–1842, BC Archives, MS 2751.

Nielsen, Steffen Bohni. "Civilizing Kwakiutl: Contexts and Contests of Kwakiutl Personhood, 1880-1999." Ph.D. diss., University of Aarhus, Denmark, 2000.

Proctor, Bill and Yvonne Maximchuk. *Full Moon, Flood Tide*. Madeira Park, BC: Harbour Publishing, 2003.

Reksten, Terry. *A Century of Sailing, 1892–1992: A History of the Oldest Yacht Club on Canada's Pacific Coast*. Victoria, BC: Orca Book Publishers, 1992.

Saanich Peninsula and Gulf Islands Review, Obituary of Muriel Wylie Blanchet, October 4, 1961.

Saint Andrews Historical Society, Bicentennial Committee, eds. *Heritage Highlights of Cornwall Township*. Cornwall: Minutemen Press, 1984.

Scull, John, chairman. *The Kingfisher*, Fall 2003. The Land Trust Alliance of British Columbia.

Segger, Martin and Douglas Franklin. *The Buildings of Samuel Maclure: In Search of Appropriate Form*. Victoria, BC: Sono Nis Press, 1986.

Sewid-Smith, Daisy Mayanił. 1997. "The Continuing Reshaping of Our Ritual World by Academic Adjuncts." *Anthropological and Education Quarterly*. (28:4) 594–602.

Spilsbury, Jim. *Spilsbury's Album: Photographs and Reminiscences of the BC Coast*. Madeira Park, BC: Harbour Publishing, 1999.

Spradley, James P. *Guests Never Leave Hungry: The Autobiography of James Sewid, a Kwakiutl Indian*. New Haven, MA: Yale University Press, 1960.

Taylor, Jeanette. *River City: A History of Campbell River and the Discovery Islands*. Madeira Park, BC: Harbour Publishing, 1999.

The Globe and Mail. "Insolvent Notice: C.A. Liffiton and The Acme Spice and Coffee Mills." October 22, 1900.

To The Totem Forests: Emily Carr and Contemporaries Interpret Coastal Villages. Peter Macnair and Jay Stewart, curators, 1998. Published in conjunction with the travelling exhibition *To The Totem Forests*, shown first at the Art Gallery of Greater Victoria, BC, August 5–October 31, 1999.

Transportation Safety Board of Canada. "TSB Statistical Summary Marine Occurrences 2005." Gatineau, Quebec, 2005.

Vodden, Kelly. "Adapting to Uncertain Futures: Alert Bay Community Background Report." Draft for Community Review. CCIAP Adapting to Uncertain Futures Project, September 2006.

Waggoner Cruising Guide, 2007: The Complete Boating Reference. Bellevue, WA: Robert Hale and Company, Weatherly Press Division, 2005.

White, Howard and Jim Spilsbury. *Spilsbury's Coast: Pioneer Years in the Wet West.* Madeira Park, BC: Harbour Publishing, 1987.

Wirsén, C.D., Permanent Secretary of the Swedish Academy. Presentation Speech upon awarding the Nobel Prize in Literature to Maurice Maeterlinck in 1911 in *Nobel Lectures, Literature 1901-1967*, ed. Horst Frenz. Amsterdam: Elsevier Publishing Company, 1969.

Yeadon-Jones, Anne and Laurence Yeadon-Jones. *Voyage of the Dreamspeaker: Vancouver-Desolation Sound Cruising Highlights.* Madeira Park, BC: Harbour Publishing, 2003.

Websites

Aboriginal Canada Portal. http:www.aboriginalcanada.gc.ca/acp/site.nsf/en-frames/index.html

Beaulieu, Viateur, Cacouna, QC: Porcupine Country, 2000–2007. http://cacouna.net/index_e.htm

Brown, Patty. Anglican Church Records in Montreal 1760–2000. St. Paul's Anglican Church 1883–1899. http://www.rootsweb.com/~qcmtl-w/AngCHrecords.html

Canada. Department of Indian and Northern Affairs. http:www.ainc-inac.gc.ca

———. "First Nation Profiles." http://sdiprod2.inac.gc.ca/FNProfiles

Canadian Hydrographic Survey. "West Coast: 1890-1973." Friends of Hydrography. Supported in collaboration with the Canadian Hydrographic Association. http://www.canfoh.org

CBC. "The St. Lawrence Seaway: Gateway to the World." CBC Archives, 2006. http://archives.cbc.ca/IDD-1-69-637/life_society.seaway

Dionne, Lynda, George Pelletier, et al. Essaies sur l'histoire Civile et Social de Cacouna. Cacouna, QC, 1975. http://cacouna.net

Finkelstein, David. "The Rise and Fall of the House of Blackwood's Magazine." Queen Margaret University College Edinburgh, UK. http://www.qmuc.ac.uk/mcs/mcc/Blackwoods

Integrated Land Management Bureau. BC Geographical Names Information System (BCGNIS). Master Database for British Columbia Place Names. http://ilmbwww.gov.bc.ca/bcnames/g2_search_options.htm

Liffiton, Thomas. "Meet Muriel W. Liffiton And M. Wylie Blanchet." http://www.Liffiton.net

Lost Villages Historical Society. "Lost Villages." http://www.lostvillages.ca/en/html/lost_villages.html

Mount Royal Cemetery. Outremont, Quebec. http://www.mountroyalcem.com

Parks Canada. "Lachine Canada National Historic Site of Canada." National Historic Sites of Canada. http://www.pc.gc.ca/lhn-nhs/qc/canallachine/active/active4a_E.asp

Stretch, Mark. "Corrosion in Salt Water Marine Engines." Old Marine Engine: A Resource for Antique Inboard Marine Engine Enthusiasts, 1999-2007. www.oldmarineengine.com/technical/corrosion_1.html

INDEX ✛

PHOTO INDEX ✛